Merge

Book Three
of the "Lola, Party of Eight" series

by
Erin Lee

*"Why should we have to give up our
lives for hers?"*
- Zoe, the dreamer

"Because she's given up hers for us."
- Maria, the mother

Dedications

*For my one true love, who reads every word
I write, no matter how crazy or "chick-like."
You understand* all *my personalities and
cherish them; every single one. It can't be
easy, but you do it flawlessly.
Thank you, from all of us.*

*For Lola Heavenkiss, who motivated this
series and continues to inspire me.
I cannot count the number of times I've
asked myself, "What would Lola do?"
I've done it. Look at me now. This is for you,
too.*

*As my youngest son would say, "Everything
happens for a reason." Sometimes, it's the
voices from those who are younger, less
experienced, or just have a different take on
life, that stay with us and are the loudest.
Jacob, we—Lola and I—heard you.
It all makes sense now: Thank you.*

Author's Note

For the third, and *final*, time:

I knew I was being a dreamer when I set out to write a series about a woman with dissociative identity disorder (DID). It's puzzling enough to write about one person's life, thoughts, hopes and dreams. Try doing it for multiple people, all in the same body. However, after months of talking to people who suffer from DID, I felt it was a challenge worth taking on. Now, on the final book of this series, I'm so glad I did.

Formerly known as multiple personality disorder and brought into pop culture after the famous Sybil case, DID is a psychological condition where portions of a person's personality split or splinter to help cope with trauma. These splits take on lives and personalities of their own, causing interesting but confusing lives for the person with the condition.

Even with my background in psychology, I've had trouble understanding what it would be like to live with multiple personalities. And, in talking to those with DID, I realize their struggles are very real; multiplied by all the personalities living in them who struggle, too. The challenges they face are bigger than I first suspected. Many people told me they don't trust therapists or others because we have such a hard time accepting their experiences. For this reason, I wanted even more to understand. I make no claim that I fully understand this disorder. However, I sympathize with those who have DID and hope Lola's story will help in spreading awareness.

In order to appreciate this condition, it's important to first know the terminology associated with DID and other, often co-occurring, pathologies. I'm including a cheat sheet to these terms to help readers make sense of some terms they may not be familiar with.

Likewise, I'm including a list of my main character—Lola's—alter egos so that readers can refer back in the event of confusion; which is bound to occur as result of the conversations, stories, and thoughts of eight (now nine) people in one body. Please refer to them as often as needed, as it's something Lola herself would do. It's not easy keeping track of so many personalities!

DID is a chronic psychological illness. A person with DID plays host to two or more personalities, called alters. Each alter has its unique way of viewing the world and may even have its own name. These personalities often take turns controlling a person's behavior.

DID occurs about eight times more frequently in women than in men and many believe that because DID can cause people to behave violently, many of the men with DID are incarcerated and undiagnosed. Women, on the other hand, are more often treated for this mental illness and end up in intense therapy and hospitalized. The average woman with DID has fifteen alters and the average man has eight. Less than three percent of people are afflicted with DID.

Many people with DID were abused as children and ultimately become so detached from reality that they begin viewing their life like another person would a television show or movie. During this state, they often go into a trance called disassociation. They can remain there indefinitely or until an alter takes over to help them live their lives. A person may or may not remember what happens when an alter is in charge of the body.

The most common DID cases take intensive therapy to treat. While there is no cure, a combination of medications and bi-weekly therapy can often resolve the symptoms of DID in about four years. However, for more extreme cases, DID requires long-term hospitalization. About five percent of DID cases are treated in psychiatric hospitals--with these cases lasting decades when there are other mental illnesses also at play.

Merge, like its predecessors *Alters* and *Host*, is a work of fiction and in no way any part of any case study or based on a real client or a real client's alters. Instead, it's a made up story about one woman facing a very real condition and written in an effort to better understand.

Reader's Guide to Dissociative Identity Disorder (DID) Terminology

DID: A chronic psychological illness. A person with DID plays host to two or more personalities called alters. Each alter has its unique way of viewing the world and may even have its own name. These personalities often take turns controlling a person's behavior as if several people were sharing the same body.

The common symptoms of DID include:

Inability to remember large parts of childhood.

Unexplained events and inability to be aware of them (such as finding yourself somewhere without remembering how you got there or having new clothes that you have no recollection of buying).

Frequent bouts of memory loss or "lost time."

Sudden return of memories, as in a flashback and/or flashback to traumatic events.

Episodes of feeling disconnected or detached from one's body and thoughts.

Hallucinations (sensory experiences that are not real, such as hearing voices talking to you or talking inside your head).

"Out of body" experiences.

Suicide attempts or self-injury.

Differences in handwriting from time to time.

Changing levels of functioning, from highly effective to nearly disabled.

People with DID may also have problems with:

Depression or mood swings.

Anxiety, nervousness, panic attacks and phobias (flashbacks, reactions to stimuli or "triggers").

Eating disorders.

Unexplained sleep problems (such as insomnia, night terrors, and sleep walking).

Severe headaches or pain in other parts of the body.

Sexual dysfunction, including sexual addiction or avoidance.

ALTER: Alternate personality that has split off or disassociated from the main personality, usually after severe childhood trauma, but not always. Also known as split, voice, alter ego, minor ego, minor.

DISASSOCIATION: Separation of a thought process or emotion from conscious awareness. Can occur when an alter is in charge of the main personality.

PERSONALITY: A group of characteristics that motivate behavior and set us apart from other individuals.

SWITCHING or SWITCH: Process by which an alternate personality, or alter, reveals itself and controls behavior.

TRAUMA: An extremely severe emotional shock.

HOST or HALTER: The primary personality and/or body carrying around one or more personalities. Also known as main, main personality, or dominant. In this series, Lola's alters refer to people with one main personality as halters, or "human alters."

MERGE: When all the alter personalities become one, dominant main personality—in effect, dying as individuals for a perceived greater good.

THE SYSTEM: The group of alter ego personalities living in a host. Sometimes, the system includes the host personality, too.

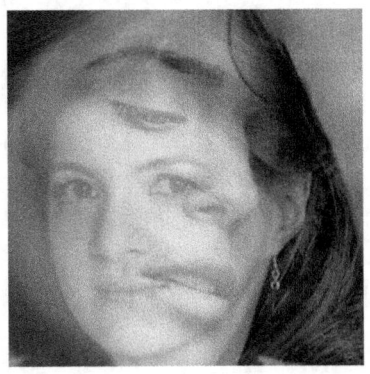

Cheat Sheet to Lola's Alters

"But there's too many of us now." –
Sam, the youngest alter

THE HOST (Personality): Lola
Murray—Age 52, suffers from paranoid
schizophrenia and dissociative identity
disorder, formerly known as multiple
personality disorder. Hospitalized thirty
years at Tillman Hospital for Mental
Wellness. Desperately seeks to find out who
she is.

ALTER (Personality) ONE: Maria—
Age 47, mother figure to the other alters.
Hopes to keep "the family" together. Strives
for peace and organization among the alters,

halters and Host. In love with the alter known as Tim.

ALTER TWO: Tim—Age 40, father figure to the other alters. Hopes to help Host escape. Wishes for independence from Host and the other alters. Serves as the family "security expert" and jack of all trades. In love with alter Maria.

ALTER THREE: Clare—Age 36, best friend to Host. Free spirit who enjoys making people laugh. Loves to entertain and refuses to be quiet.

ALTER FOUR: Zoe—Age 29, surrogate mother figure to the younger alters. A collector who thrives on drama and dreams about one day making it to the big stage. Resents Host for holding the alters hostage. Desperate to find her "one true love."

ALTER FIVE: Frog—Age 20, big brother and protector of the two youngest alters. Serves as a back-up and friend to Tim. Strives to keep other alters from emerging. Philosopher.

ALTER SIX: Rabbit—Age 14, the smartest and most tech savvy of the alters. Lonely and depressed, Rabbit wishes she could find a friend her own age. Goal is to one day be "a normal kid." However, being a suicidal cutter doesn't help with things.

ALTER SEVEN: Samantha—Age 8, the youngest and happiest of the alters. Having never lived outside a host or institution, tomboy Samantha loves her alter family and wishes things would never change, despite it being "kinda smushy in here."

ALTER EIGHT: Roy—Age 52, "The New Guy." Roy has just shown up and claims to have been in the alters' system all along. Claiming to be a surrogate father figure to Lola, who had no relationship with her biological father growing up. The other alters take exception to him only making himself known now. Regardless of tensions, Roy says he is here to stay and is the only person who has the patience and ability to make things right and help with a final merge. Or, maybe not.

Table of Contents

Chapter One
Where's Host?

"What was that?"

"You mean, *who* was that?"

Tim and Maria look at each other, unsure of where to go first--to check on Host or to investigate the system to find the owner of the strange, deep voice.

"You don't think there's another one, do you?" Maria shudders at the thought of sharing Host's body with yet another alter ego.

"There's no way…"

"There can't be. I swear, if there is, I'll kill him myself. It must have been Frog. We can worry about that later. Right now, we need to figure out what's going on with Host."

"Fair enough. How long has it been since she's moved?"

"I'm not sure. She hasn't been right since her mother died. I cannot believe that we're back here, again," Tim says, shaking his head. "We worked so hard to get out of Rosewood. Leave it to Host to put us right back where we started. I really am going to have to come up with an escape plan this time. They're never going to discharge her now. She had her chance. *We* had our chance. *She* blew it!"

"No. It will be fine. She lost her mother. It's an explainable thing. This isn't just an ordinary break. Anyone would be upset," Maria says, swallowing her guilt for how she's treated Host's mother—Stella—all these years.

"Yeah, I get that. But look at her. She's basically catatonic. That's not going to go well for us. We need to find a way to get her up and moving. It's like she's not here at all," Tim says.

"I think she's giving up."

"I know."

"We need to give her a reason to want to get up. She probably feels as guilty as I do. I mean, she didn't make her mother's life easier either."

"Be serious, Maria. She spent two decades in and out of psych wards. It's not like she could really help herself. It can't be easy being a host."

"Since when are *you* Host's number one defender?"

"Are you kidding me? I've been defending her—all of us—all these years. Don't take this out on me."

"Sorry. You're right. I'm just saying. I mean, you're the one who is always telling her to get up and put her big girl panties on.

Telling her she can do it and not to be weak."

"Yeah, it's one thing to say it. It's another thing to believe it. Do you think I don't get how hard this is for her? I know what it's like to struggle. I'm a guy in a system with one other guy and surrounded by women. I get struggle. The struggle is real." Tim laughs.

"Oh, shut up. There's no time for joking around. We really need to do something to help her. We'll be in Rosewood forever. Is that what you want?"

"Listen, Queen Obvious, I want that less than any of us! If you remember correctly, I was the one who spent all that time working up plans to get us out the first time around. How quickly you forget."

"Do you want a thank you card or something with that? I don't forget. But lighting maintenance rooms on fire isn't really the best plan. The only plan we should have is getting her better, so she can get out happy, functional, and safe."

"You're no fun today."

"You're acting twelve. If you aren't going to help me, then go hang out with Rabbit and Sam or something. I need to think." It's been months since Maria's felt this annoyed with Tim. But she can't help it. Watching Host lay in a hospital bed, again, is just too much for her. There's no time for joking. Something needs to be done, and fast.

Sensing Maria's annoyance, Tim decides to take another approach. "Okay, listen, what do you want to do?"

"Maybe I should talk to her?"

Tim shakes his head. "She isn't going to listen. I'm not sure if she's even *in* here. She may be disassociated all together and won't be able to hear you anyway."

"True. That's what happened last time."

"I think the only way to do is it to do a switch. I'm not sure who to put in charge. But if we can get her in here with us, it might be easier to figure out where she's at and get her talking. You women need to talk all the time. Talking will help her."

Maria glares at Tim, but doesn't say anything.

"Oh, come on, you know I'm right," he continues.

"Maybe we put Clare in charge? I mean, running around naked and screaming and trying to make people laugh isn't nearly as bad as laying there, half dead, right?"

"No, not Clare. Clare will make her seem even more crazy. What about Frog?"

"Frog will hit on the nurses."

"Okay, Rabbit?" As soon as he asks the question, Tim rethinks himself. "Never mind, not Rabbit, she's practically suicidal. She can't be in charge. She'll have us in an emergency room from slitting Host's wrists. If we even live to get that far."

"Zoe?"

Tim shrugs. "Maybe. But I'd worry about Dr. Ross. She's convinced he's Host's soulmate. She's sure of it."

"True. But is that so bad? I mean, what's the worst that can happen? She hits on him?"

"Bad for his career, for sure. And he's a good guy. He doesn't need more problems than we've already caused."

"I thought you hated him."

"Why is it that only women are allowed to change their minds?"

"Why are you so sexist?"

"I'm not sexist! Not even a little!"

"Yeah. Right."

***

Zoe

It's adorable—said sarcastically—how Maria and Tim think they have a say about everything. Maria and Tim. Tim and Maria. For people who say they don't believe in soulmates, they sure do bicker like an old married couple. I mean, be serious, people. Do they think I can't hear them? My name isn't Host. I don't split or run at the first sign of trouble. Nope. Not this girl. I'm going to take matters in my own hands. While they figure out what to do, I'm actually going to *do* something.

They are right. I do think Dr. Ross is our soulmate. And it's wrong, what's happening to him. Some people figured it was cool to gossip and say he did something wrong with Host by taking her to her mother's funeral and stuff. Spending too much time with her. Whatever. I can't imagine what they will think of our wedding. But I'm getting ahead of myself. For now, I have work to do.

I'm already at the helm. I've switched into Host while the others think she's sleeping or in a coma or disassociating or whatever they want to call it. I figured, why not? The difference between me and the other alters is that I *do* have a plan. I have all along. I promise, it's the best plan in the world.

My plan is to get Dr. Ross in here. To make the nurses and staff believe he is the only person who can help Host. When I have him where I need him, I'll convince him that we are right for each other. I know he likes us. He's made that clear. Why else would he risk his career to help us? I mean, it can't be straight client loyalty, can it? No other doctor or shrink has taken such an interest in us. There *has* to be more. I know it. I can *feel* it.

The first thing I need to do is get Host looking better. The doctor can't see her looking like this. She's been out of it for weeks. She will be so happy when she finally does come back and realizes she's happy, with Dr. Ross, and living free again in the world. Of course, she'll have to take turns with me. I am not going anywhere any time soon. Not as long as that man walks the planet!

Normally, I don't have a lot of time in charge. This time is different. There's a new guy in here. I saw him myself. Seems nice enough. I didn't talk to him. At first, he scared me. But he seemed friendly. For now, I'm keeping that on the down-low. Another alter is going to be enough to keep Tim and Maria busy and distracted for months. Maybe he will give Clare something to do too. He's kind of handsome. If it wasn't for Dr. Ross, I might just go back inside and try flirting with him. I'm a really good flirt. I've read how to do it in *Cosmo* and I've even practiced on Sam and Frog.

I've been studying everything. I read an article about how to get a man to fall in love with you. I'm all over it. I have the entire thing memorized and I plan to use each of the bullet items to my benefit. Dr. Ross won't know what hit him. Neither will the others, not with this new guy around.

I wish I could tell Clare what I'm up to. She does the best job on Host's make-up. I can't because she has a big mouth. I need them to think I'm just busy and stay distracted. They can say all day that it's my time to be in charge, but I'm not buying it. They'd change their minds the minute they caught on to my plan. That's what they do. It's also why nothing ever gets done, not with Maria and Tim in charge.

If I could talk to Clare, I'd ask her how the heck to get these knots out of Host's hair. I can't understand how they got here. I can't get up. If I do, it will alert Tim and Maria that something is different. But there's no way I can let Dr. Ross see me this way.

Today, once I figure out how to look decent, I'll call Dr. Ross and ask him to visit. I'll promise him that it will only be quick and that he's the only one who can help me. I'll promise him a merge. His one flaw is that he thinks we should merge. He's wrong there, but he will change his mind and see the value in keeping us—all of us—intact.

Marrying us will be a great adventure; eight, or nine, for the price of one. He'll be able to shrink us forever. He'll never get bored. I mean, what more could a psychiatrist want? He'll agree with me, eventually, they'll see.

Chapter Two
The New Guy

Roy

My name is Roy. I'm the 'new' alter ego. The thing is, I'm not new at all. In fact, I've been here all along. Sometimes, that's the best way; watching, learning, doing and saying nothing. Not until you have a plan. I'll agree with Zoe on that.

I came around before the others. I came around when Host's biological father—the "sperm donor" is what the other alters call him—left her and her mother. Now, with her mother gone, I need to make myself known. Every kid needs a parent. Even when they are middle-aged, like Host. Maria can say she's Host's "true' mother", but the truth is, her mother was Stella. And, God, do I miss that woman. I'm not even sure why. Most of the time, she made me crazy.

Crazy—the bad kind—must be very contagious. Stella was nuts, just like the donor. It's true. I won't lie about that. *Note to self: I should probably stop using that word.* But she wasn't nuts in the sort of way that should make a man leave the mother of his child. You see, Host's biological father was Stella's boss. They had an affair and he begged her to have an abortion, so his wife wouldn't find out. Well, part of him did. It's complicated.

As nuts as she was, Stella told him she was keeping the baby. She'd raise her alone if she had to. And, for the most part, that's exactly what she did until she met Travis – Host's stepfather.

Backing up, Host's biological father wasn't that bad when you look at the big picture. I mean, I can see his point of view. One of them, anyway. Originally, he told Stella that he only wanted a fling. Hell, Stella used to take calls from his wife. Later, she'd take messages, even, in a sweet voice that would make you sick; knowing she had a six-month-old at home. She insisted that she was the only person who *truly* understood him. She called him her one true love. She sounded a lot like Zoe, actually. I can't say I don't have a soft spot for that, or for Zoe--a sweetheart. Maybe it's why I miss Stella. Anyway, he tried for that first year to be in Host's life. It just wasn't meant to be. I mean, he had a whole other life, a few of them, actually.

I've kept an eye on him over the years, during moments where Host and the others were sleeping. He lost his wife in 2006 and had been trying to hook up with Stella ever since. She wouldn't say much more to him than that the ship had sailed. I think he regretted it, not following his heart and leaving his wife for her. But that's the risk you run; playing with people's hearts. He was at her funeral. Host and the others were clueless. But seeing him, standing there, crying over Stella's coffin and staring at Host, I knew it was time to finally make myself known. I have a feeling Host will be hearing from him soon. Someone's going to need to step in. That's where I'll come in. Stella isn't around to protect her. And Tim and Maria are too distracted to notice. I need to prepare everyone. So, here goes.

***

"Hello."

"What the fuck? Who the hell are *you*?" Frog jumps up, not sure whether to punch or extend a hand to what appears to be a new alter in the system. He clenches his fists and cracks his knuckles. *Pop. Pop. Pop.*

"I'm Roy. I mean no harm. Relax, Frog."

"Roy? What? Who *are* you? How long have you been in here?"

"I've been here all along."

"Bullshit. What do you want from us? And how do you know my name?"

"I told you, dude. I've been here all along. I know *all* of you. I am *one* of you."

"Does Host know this?"

"No."

"What are you doing here then? And why now? Is this 'cause her mother died?"

"No. And, I just told you. I've been here all along. I was the first."

"Yeah, right, dude. You were the first."

"I was! Ask me anything. I can give you an answer. A date even."

"What's Host's birthday?"

"September 8, 1969."

"You could have read that somewhere. What's the name of the youngest alter?"

"Samantha. Sam, for short."

"What's Tim's birthday?"

"November. November 16th."

Frog wants to wipe the smug look off the new guy's face. "Let me get this straight. You have been in the system all these years—longer than Maria—and no one has known you were here? Where have you been hiding? And why? What kind of psycho even does that?"

Roy sighs. Taking a deep breath, he begins, "Look, I'm not the enemy here. I'm no more psycho than any of you are. I came here when Host's biological father left her. Do you think a bad haircut was enough to start this whole thing off? And, if you have done any reading at all, you will also realize that this kind of thing runs in families. She was predisposed to it. Some halters have alters with no issues at all."

"I really don't need a presentation on DID. I'm asking you why you have never made yourself known before."

Roy shrugs. "Why would I have? My job was to make sure she was okay. I did that."

"You think she's okay, dude? I mean, look at her. She's just lying in a hospital bed, again. You're no better than her sperm donor. You came to replace her father? Give me a break. You sound as bad as Maria and Tim. She—we—have enough authority figures in our lives, thanks."

"Look, I hear what you are saying. I really do. And I know she's in a bad place right now. That's why I'm here. Her mother's gone and Tim and Maria are too busy flirting with each other to be of much use. Someone had to step in. Do *you* really want to be in charge? You can send me a thankyou note later, after I fix this situation."

"Yeah, sure, dude. Maybe you ought to go talk to Tim and see what *he* thinks of this. I have a feeling he and Maria—distracted or not—aren't about to give up the helm. In fact, let's find out."

Frog blows a loud whistle, one so loud that alters come running to the pons, where he and Roy have been talking. The first to arrive are Sam, Clare and Rabbit.

Rabbit crosses her arms over her chest, first glaring at Frog, then at Roy. "Great, another one. And why do you have to be so darn loud? I was trying to concentrate."

"We need to have a meeting," Frog says. "This guy—he points to Roy—thinks he is in charge. Says he's been here all along. Have you ever seen him before?"

Sam shakes her head and reaches for Rabbit's arm. She hides behind the older alter.

"Nope. And, frankly, Frog, I don't have the time or interest to get to know another new person. No offense, sir," Rabbit says.

"None taken, Rabbit. I already know you: All of you. I'm Roy, and I'm pleased to meet you officially."

Rabbit grunts.

"How do you already know her? I don't get it. Are you like Peter Pan?" Sam asks, curling around Rabbit's arm.

"I keep trying to tell you people that I've been here all along." Roy says, curtly. Then, he softens. "Sorry. I'm not trying to be mean. Yes, in a way, I'm like Peter Pan. But different. I know things."

"But how?"

"I just do. It's like magic. You believe in magic, right, Sam?"

"Yes. And how do you know my name?"

"I told you: Magic."

"Ohhhh! He's *cool*! Can we keep him, Rabbit?"

Rabbit grunts again, just as Maria and Tim enter the pons. Clare is the first to speak.

"Look at this shit. This guy, Roy, says he's a new alter but that he's not new, ya'll. And he's trying to take charge or something, right, Frog?"

"Who the hell are *you*?" Tim demands.

"That's what I said," Frog says. "And what took you so long?"

"Hi Tim. I'm Roy. The first alter."

"Umm, no. Maria is the first alter."

"That's right. I am."

Roy shakes his head. "You came around when Host was in the first grade. I was here long before that—1970. I just didn't say anything."

"Look, guys, you may not want to hear this, but here goes. I need you to pay attention. I don't want to run through this ten times. Is everyone listening?"

"Zoe's not here."

"Oh, who cares. She's probably sleeping. She's been depressed. I'll fill her in later. I want to hear this. This shit is gonna be good, ya'll," Clare says, batting her eyelashes at Roy and flipping her hair.

"I told you, this stuff runs in families, right? Well, that definitely applies in Host's family. Her father—sperm donor—actually had DID too. It was one of his alters who had an affair with her mother. Stella, well, she was as crazy as anyone and…"

"See? I *told* you she was crazy!" Maria says, "…Not to talk ill of the dead or anything but…"

"Stella wasn't crazy in *that* way. Host's father was. He had DID. And can we stop calling it crazy, please? That just makes us crazy and that drives me nuts; pun intended. If Host wasn't, as you love to call it, 'crazy,' we wouldn't even exist," Roy says.

"Jesus, dude. Enough with the lecture. You should know that crazy isn't a bad thing around these parts. Had you really actually been around all these years, you'd know that," Frog says.

Roy shakes his head in disgust. Then, he continues: "Anyway, Host's father was married. He was her mother's boss…"

"Should Sam really be hearing this?"

"How's it going to hurt her? She's going to find out anyway. It's not like we can send her to the park. And she's as much a part of us as any of us."

Except you, Clare muses.

"Okay, I guess."

"Her father had five alters, from what I can gather. One of them—Henry—is who Stella fell in love with. They really *were* in love. And for a year or so, they were able to pull it off. But when Henry's host found out, and eventually his system merged, that was the end of that and Stella was left on her own.

"Wow, that's scandal!" Clare screams, causing Maria to jump.

"I don't buy it," Tim says. "Too easy."

"Me either. If you'd been around all these years, you'd have said something or done something by now," Maria adds. "What kind of man are you, anyway?"

"The kind of man who knows when to keep his mouth shut," Roy says. "Some of you should try it. Really."

Chapter Three
Crazy Love

Dr. Aaron Ross has reminded himself not to skip when he walks since meeting Lola a year ago. For the first time in a decade, he feels energized. He wants to change something, everything. Anything. Earlier today, he'd even toyed with the idea of shaving his furry face before heading to the office but decided against it. That would be just as obvious as caving to his temptation to dye his hair to mask its slight hints of gray, he'd decided. He senses Lola would pick up on something like that even with her in her current state. With winter knocking, he'll soon appreciate the warmth a beard provides, anyway. Plus, he remembers how Caroline had always hated his beard. He'd see her soon on one of his daughter, Sage's, college tour visits. *It will piss her off. She can't make me shave it now. Beard stays.*

He'd wished, for years, that things could be cordial between him and his ex-wife but considered himself a realist. The pair had separated when Sage was in the first grade after several years of daily squabbles over everything from who was in charge of laundry to whose turn it was to take out the trash. In fact, intensive couples and individual therapy—on his dime, of course—had shown him that the only reason he'd agreed to have a second child, Abby, was in hopes that a new baby might bring balance back to the family. He should have known better, he supposed, being a psychiatrist and all. But it's hard to see your own issues objectively. While he'd never regret his youngest child and still disliked odd numbers, he wished he hadn't spent so many years trying to fix an unfixable situation. At least he'd learned he wasn't afraid to commit. That's what he reminded himself, over and over, as he wrote out checks for Caroline's nails and missed out on tucking his daughters in at night. As he did this, he often thought about what it was like for Lola, not having her real father around. He also understood her regrets about missing so much time being trapped in a nuthouse; it's how his marriage had felt.

Over the years, he'd tried to be as involved in his daughters' lives as possible. He'd been at every softball and field hockey game. He was already on the volunteer list to chaperone Sage's Project Graduation party, a gesture Caroline insisted was "typical" and somehow forced her to roll her eyes. He was the one who funded extras like pink cleats and prom dresses he still didn't have pictures of. Despite the hefty child support he had deducted from his weekly check, he'd even sent Caroline extra money to be sure she could keep their daughters in the house they'd been born in. No one would ever be able to truthfully say that he wasn't doing all that he could for his girls, except Caroline; but that was a given.

He'd never forgive himself for missing Abby's birth because Caroline was too mad to let him in the room. He'd promised himself to be the best father he could be from afar; even though he'd never pictured himself parenting every other weekend instead of daily. *It doesn't matter now. Soon, the girls will be out of there, and I will be as free as them. Caroline won't have any control at all.*

As he pulls up mental wellness grant writing software on his laptop, he tells himself not to daydream and to focus on his work. It isn't going to be easy. He's looking specifically for a grant on DID research; something he could use to help Lola. He still can't understand why he was so drawn to— fascinated by—her. While the word "writing" is in the title of the task at hand, it isn't the kind of writing he enjoys. Instead, he prefers writing short stories with grim details of ghostly towns in New England where murders were carried out on long windy roads with lonely, sleepy houses. He wonders if Lola would ever consider attending a writers' group meeting. He contemplates what the eclectic bunch of regulars would think of his favorite client. *You're getting ahead of yourself. Stop. You aren't allowed to date a client for at least two years post treatment. And what state will she be in by then anyway? Keep it together. Just focus on trying to help her.*

Despite his better judgment, he lets his mind drift anyway. It would certainly give the group something to gossip about, he decides. The group has been getting a little stale and could use some shaking up. A new member—especially one with so many personalities and quirks—always helps with new plot ideas and twist endings. He could lie to himself and say it would only be platonic, but the truth is that he isn't hoping she'd show up for anything but his own selfish reasons. It's been so long since he's even been interested in a woman. Between the girls' hectic weekend schedules and his efforts to show up at all school events, even on weekdays, there isn't much time for a social life. Frankly, after the bitter divorce with Caroline, he wasn't sure he would ever be ready for a serious relationship again. But something about Sage graduating soon gives him a sense of hope; like a first chapter of a new book.

Sure, it had been more than a decade. And there had been dates and one night stands along the way. But Aaron just can't see himself committing to one person again, not if he was really honest with himself. The truth is, he's been afraid it'd turn out the way it had with Caroline and doesn't want to be responsible for more heartache in the world. Even when he writes his short stories, he tries to stay off the topic of love and rarely gives his protagonists love interests. *With Lola, it would be different. And, technically, Pezanowski will be her doctor of record anyway.*

Oddly, he feels a sudden urge to try writing in a new genre—romance—and closes the grant file. He isn't in the mood to pull up his novel. It's too gritty for his good mood. He opens a new document and begins a fresh story: *Dreamers.*

Excited to try something new, he tells himself he can catch up later—one of the benefits of his flexible job. *Screw it. I can write about the need for more funding in the new psych program and DID in general later. It's not like that's going to go away. ...I wonder how she's doing. I wish I could find out. But if I call there, it would look bad. They are still questioning me about why I took her to Stella's funeral. Ethics board from hell. Who wouldn't need support after something like that? They have to make everything seem so ill-intentioned. Stop. Don't think about it. Just write. Escape reality.*

It is well past noon before Aaron looks up from his screen. His stomach growls as a reminder that it's time to take a break. He wants to get home to feed Rocky anyway. Rocky, Aaron's ten-year-old Siberian Husky, has been his best and only real friend since the divorce was finalized. Of course, Sage and Abby are there, but he can hardly call his daughters friends. His job is to parent, not befriend, them and he takes that responsibility seriously.

Aaron purposely takes the long way— past the Rosewood lockdown wing—to the parking lot. He knows Lola 's schedule by heart and feels guilty about it. She'd never believe he just happened to be in the group therapy wing if he ran into her but isn't sure he cares. From what he's heard, she isn't doing much walking around anyway. *She's probably not even in group. She's not ready for that.* Or, maybe seeing him would help her, he decides. In fact, he suspects she might feel flattered if she knew he was trying to create opportunities for another run in. Still, there is a part of him that feels like a stalker. *She probably thinks I'm too old for her anyway. To her, I'm just another dumb*

*old doctor. Just be happy with the time you
do get with her and try to help her.*

He hurries his pace and races the full four
minutes home in time to wake Rocky from
his nap. His house is cheerful yet
unremarkable, exactly the opposite of the
houses he likes to write about. Set at the east
end of a busy neighborhood, it is a deep
green that matches the summer moss that
curls around the chimney every July like
clockwork. It has a modest driveway,
complimented by planters—currently filled
with mums struggling to survive in the final
days of autumn—on either side. He checks
the mailbox before pulling in and finds
nothing but bills and coupons from the local
sports equipment store where he often buys
the girls' birthday and Christmas presents.

Rocky, gray in the muzzle but filled with
endless energy for a dog his age, greets him
with licks and a wagging tail and promptly
heads to his food bowl. He looks at his
master expectantly; appreciating that Aaron
is also a creature of habit.

"Well, you were hungry," Aaron says,
checking his silver watch. "You're usually
on your third nap by now, Rock."

The dog gobbles down his meal as Aaron
pours himself a glass of cider and nibbles on
carrot sticks with ranch dressing from the
fridge. He sits at the kitchen table,

wondering what to make for lunch, as he glances at his laptop. Tempted to call in sick for the rest of the day, so he can write without distraction, he pushes the laptop away and gets up to make a tuna sandwich. He'd set a goal to finish chapter four of his latest novel, *The Game*, in time for writers' group critique this week and is mad at himself for making no progress. Lately, he's just been in a funk with the book. Writer's block happens to all writers. He knows it too well. He hadn't been able to write for years after his divorce. But he'd long since gotten over that and can't understand what the holdup is now. He wishes for a muse and decides maybe his problem is that he just isn't into the topic anymore. Lately, he prefers writing shorter pieces. He likes how it feels to complete something and isn't up for the two-year marathon writing a novel takes as opposed to the sprint of a poem or short story.

Stop being so critical of yourself. You'll get back to it. Don't beat yourself up over it. Treat yourself the way you tell Lola to treat herself. Wonder what idea's she'd have. Hope she's feeling better. This is hell, not knowing.

So far, *The Game* is the story of a man haunted by a ghost from his past. The ghost has been resurrected to get revenge on the man; who had wronged him nearly three decades ago. But something about writing about revenge and justice doesn't feel as satisfying these days, now that he is over the pain of his divorce and has settled into a rhythm with his new, self-made life. He is finishing off his sandwich when his cell phone rings. He smiles when he sees his oldest daughter's name.

"What's up, hon?" he asks Sage.

"I have to sign up to retake the SAT's. Mom said to call you for a check. It's due today. Can you drop it off at the school?"

Aaron holds back his groan. It isn't his daughter's fault that Caroline doesn't understand the purpose of child support. And taking the SAT's for a second time is really important for her. Never a good test taker, Sage had still managed to earn straight A's and has her heart set on attending college at UCLA. With application deadlines looming, Aaron knows she needs this to bring that dream to fruition.

Gee. Thanks for the notice. "Sure, hon. Do I just drop it off at the office?"

"Yep. Just leave it with the secretary up front," Sage says. "Thanks, Dad."

He notices Abby's history book on the kitchen table as Sage finishes her check-writing and drop off instructions. *At least I can drop that off, too. Does Caroline ever do* anything *for these kids?*

Aaron reminds himself that the kids wouldn't be kids much longer as he gulps down the rest of his lemonade and jumps back into his car. *So much for being sick the rest of the day.* Rocky stares out the bay window, as if to say "where are you going so soon?"

***

It is nearly 2 p.m. when Aaron finally returns to his office. This time, he forces himself to look at the grant application. He doesn't allow himself to be distracted by anything else—including short stories, his orphan novel, and fantasies of the one and only Lola Murray.

Three hours later, he is unsuccessful. Not only does he find himself right back into *Dreamers*—debating the hair color of the protagonist—but he can't get Lola out of his head. There is something about her. Her eyes are mysterious and that it could only be because of a secret she is still hiding. *Or is it sadness? Fear? They are curious, too. Looking for something. What? Is it the alters I'm seeing?* He still remembers the way Lola looked up at him during their first meeting. He hadn't been able to take the deer-in-headlight expression out of his mind ever since. She reminded him of Bambi and he felt an odd desire to protect her instantly.

He double checks the mental health board's policy on doctor/client relationships before deciding he isn't going to be able to concentrate on anything work-related for the rest of the day. Grateful that it is only a paperwork day and that he doesn't have clients, he turns his attention elsewhere. Thoughts of his age—old enough to have a daughter heading to college in under a year—trigger Aaron to remember Sage's college application essay. He dedicates the rest of the afternoon to working on her common application. It's hard to believe his little girl is old enough to even be applying. He knows he should be making her do it herself, but he can't help himself. It's no different than how he is with Lola. *I won't be able to help either of them forever.* Sometimes, he wishes he could stop time. But lately, he's felt itchy for the freedom and liberation that having independent children will mean.

Stay in the present. You still have to get Abby through. It's a trick his own therapist had helped him with during the darkest days of his divorce. While Aaron watched Caroline take everything material from him, what he most struggled with was the loss of his family unit. He felt like a failure, and it was helpful, he'd eventually admitted, to focus on the task at hand instead of looking too far into an uncertain future. *What would Lola do? Bless the past and move forward. That's what she always says. I think Ann taught her that.*

He scratches his forehead as he puts the final touches on Sage's essay— "(Not So) Ordinary Ambitions"—and sends it to her school email address hoping she'll have a chance to check on it during her study hall. Then, he texts Abby to go to the front office for her textbook. He won't see either of them for a few days. While he is used to the on again, off again schedule, he simply wishes it didn't have to be this way. It feels, well, empty.

Maybe it would be easier with Lola around. Stop thinking about her. It can't happen. You are better than that. You'd never want to hurt her. You care about her. It wouldn't be right. Just stay as far away as you can get. The others can help her. Pezanowski is a great doctor.

***

Zoe isn't fazed by the obstacles presented with being back in Rosewood. Instead, she sees the swarming nurses, med calls, and

44

machinery as simply more obstacles she will overcome. Nothing will stand in the way of her and the system's one true love. She's spent the day convincing doctors and nurses that she's feeling better. She's asked for phone privileges under the guise of wanting to check up on Host's step-father and sister. She will get them, she's been told, so long as she participates in group therapy today. She's agreed—likely too easily, she concludes—and is the first to arrive.

The group therapy room has been renovated since the last time Zoe acted as the main personality. Gone are the plastic chairs, replaced with plush couches and overstuffed loveseats. She's tempted to take a nap. Instead, she practices what she will say when she's finally able to get that phone call. With a plan to convince Dr. Aaron Ross to visit her, she knows she'll need to have her best game face on. It won't be easy. But not even he will stop her, she concludes. *It's too important to the system.*

"You're back?" Justin, a chubby young man with Downs Syndrome and anger management issues stands in the doorway. "I thought you were outta here?"

"Hi Justin," Zoe says, doing her best to mimic Host's usual stoic tone. "Yeah. You know how it is. In. Out. In. Out."

"They never let me out. They just leave me here. I don't know how I'm supposed to get a girlfriend. Tina still doesn't want me." Justin walks toward Zoe. "You're in my chair. You gotta move."

"Oh, sorry. They changed stuff."

"Yup."

Zoe moves to a couch opposite the chair Justin has claimed. It's silly, she decides, how they've arranged furniture this big into a circle. She prefers the old arrangement. *At least the plastic chairs didn't take up so much space and the room felt bigger. Whatever. We won't be here long. Soon, we'll be arranging loveseats at home with Dr. Ross.* "So, Tina's still here, hugh?"

"Yup."

Tina, Host's former roommate, has also been in and out of Rosewood for most of her life. A self-harmer with many suicide attempts under her belt, the young girl hates it at Rosewood more than most of Host's alters. "That sucks. How's she doing?"

"She's just Tina. She won't give me the time of day. Shocker."

Zoe nods, wishing Justin had been dealt a different hand in life, as a group of both familiar and unfamiliar faces walks in. She recognizes Lindsay, a spoiled woman in her 50's with a shopping addiction and endless trust fund from her late parents; Huey, a big-hearted schizophrenic; Edna, an elderly woman with the worst case of anxiety Zoe's ever seen; and Tom, who suffers from severe bipolar disorder. They take turns firing questions at her while they wait for the perpetually late therapist—Ann—to arrive. *Some things never change.*

***

Two hours later, Zoe wishes she could convince Host's hands to stop shaking as she dials Dr. Ross's office number. The three rings it takes him to answer go off in her head like gunshots, flooding Host's body with fear and excitement. *I can't let the others hear me. They wouldn't like this.*

"Hello?"

"Hi, Dr. Ross. It's me, Zo, Lo-Lola." *Dammit, you practiced this. Idiot.*

"Lola? Lola Murray?"

"Yes. It's me."

There's a long pause.

"Lola, you know I'm not supposed to be speaking with you. I'm making a referral for you. People think it wasn't appropriate. … Never mind. How are you? Are you doing okay?"

"Who cares what people think?"

"I do."

"Why? It's not true. Right?"

"Of *course* it's not true. I've told you. This relationship is strictly doctor/patient. I would never do anything to get in the way of your recovery."

"Of course not. So there's no big deal. The thing is, you're the only one I trust."

"I know. Trust takes time. Trust is hard."

"Dr. Ross, don't give me the shrink talk. I'm being serious."

"I am too."

"I need your help."

"You need to talk to Ann and the new psychiatrist. Have you seen him yet?"

"No. I just got up today. I've been out of it. You're the only one I want to talk to." Zoe clears Host's throat. She waves at orderly Brown, who looks as surprised to see her as Justin did.

"How are you feeling?"

"I feel like I need to talk to you."

"You're talking to me now."

"No, in person."

"Lola, that's not a good idea."

"Look, Dr. Ross. If I could, I'd come visit you. But I can't see them letting me leave. Please? It would really help me," Zoe says, softening her voice. "Please? Pretty please?"

"Fine. I'll come see how you're doing on one condition."

"What's that?"

"That you hook up with this psychiatrist I'm referring you to and really do the work. I can't always be there, Lola. That's not how this works. Promise me you will give him a chance."

"Deal," Zoe squeals. *The only one I'm hooking up with is you, Dr. Aaron Ross. Zoe Ross. Mrs. Aaron Ross. Has a nice ring to it. Yes!*

"I mean it, Lola. I have a license to protect and a career. I have people watching me."

God, I hate it when he calls me that. It would be so nice to hear him say my name. Zoe. Just Zoe. Not Lola. Not anyone else. Just Zoe. "I know you mean it and they are the ones who should be watched, not you. You've done nothing wrong. It's ridiculous. Thank you, Dr. Ross! You will never know how much this means to…"

"I need to go, my daughter just walked in. She needs some help with an assignment for cultural studies."

"Okay. I'll see you soon?"

"Yes. See you soon. And, please, take care of yourself."

"I will! Bye!"

Chapter Four
Three's a Crowd

"Look, buddy, you need to understand something. It doesn't matter how long you have been here. Facts are facts. You didn't bother to make you presence known. What kind of man does that? Not this one. I just don't get you, and I have no interest in listening to all this shit about the sperm donor. It is what it is. You aren't helping things and the last thing we all need is another person to cram into this place. Can't you make like a tree and leave or something? You know, go missing for another half century?" Tim is tempted to physically fight Roy. Never has he wished more for an actual body to do it with. But a fight can't happen inside a female host between two male personalities. *I can't even ask him to step outside. I fucking hate this.*

Roy stares at Tim, then chuckles. "Are you done?"

"No. I'm not even close to done. You just don't get it, do you?"

"No, I guess I don't. I don't see what the problem is. You did things your way, I'm doing them mine. I would think you'd be glad to have another guy around here to help even things out. What's the issue?"

"Yeah, that might have been nice all this time, but not now."

"Afraid of a little competition?"

"What? What the fuck does that mean?"

"Oh, you know, with Maria, Zoe, Clare. The ladies."

"Are you fucking serious?" Tim could kill. He's never felt so angry. Not even the time in the bar fight.

"You wouldn't have a shot with a single woman in here. They aren't about to trust a coward."

"Really?"

"Really. Now leave me the fuck alone."

"How am I a coward?"

"Get the fuck out of here, dude. I'm serious."

"What are you going to do about it?"

"What is all this yelling about?" Maria pushes past Tim into the center of the pons. "You boys need to chill out! Zoe is in charge, and we promised to keep everyone calm. What is the problem in here?"

"This mother fucker thinks he has a chance with you," Tim yells.

Maria laughs. "What?"

Tim smiles and nods at Roy. "See?"

Roy smiles back. "I don't think that's why she was laughing."

"Oh, please! Both of you, stop! I have no interest in either of you at the moment. You are acting like children and disrupting the entire system. We don't need this right now. Cut it out!"

"She has a point," Roy says.

"Sure. Kiss her ass. That turns her on. Whatever, dude."

"I'm not kissing her ass. I've been saying this all day. We need to work together. We all need to be on the same team here. You know, united."

"Where were you when the team needed unity all these years?"

"Not *that* again. I told you. Everyone has a different way of leading. I didn't think we needed more confusion."

"Boys! Drop it. This isn't helping." Maria commands.

"Call me a boy again, Maria. Do it."

"You know what I mean! Just stop. Tim is right. I don't have much respect for how you have made your presence known out of the blue. It's not helping anything. If you wanted to be known, you should have come forward like the rest of us; in the beginning. All that time and I thought I was the only one? You were there all along? Disgusting."

"Or, respectful. To you and to Host. I, unlike any of you, felt she deserved to have her own life. It's not her fault her father passed on a mental illness. Had any of you—all of you—respected that too, she'd have a normal life. Has anyone thought of that?"

Silence. And then: "…Wow. No. I hadn't," Maria says. "I'm a horrible person."

"No, you aren't! You were trying to help her. We all were," Tim says. "Fine, what is your plan, Roy? And it better be good…"

***

Clare

Maria and Tim can argue with Roy all day long. But someone needs to stop Zoe. There is no way, no possible way, that adding a love affair with Dr. Ross is going to make our situation any easier, ya'll.

They say I'm the one who causes problems. They say all I care about is making jokes and being up on stage. Well, they are wrong. What I care about is getting us the heck out of Rosewood and not complicating matters with some snobby doctor type none of us can trust anyway. If Zoe wants to find true love, she can do it on her own time.

I cannot believe that they—the three oldest and supposedly leaders—are really going to make me do this. Like Zoe and I don't argue enough. I get to be the one to stop her? Great. That will do wonders for our relationship. Have they forgotten the five-year silent treatment all because Zoe felt I was stealing the show? This is going to be a blast, ya'll.

In the end, it will somehow be me—Clare, the trouble maker—who caused the problems. No one will remember that they were too busy bickering to stop the love addict from ruining a man's career and ending our chances of ever leaving the nut house. Nope. It will just be "Clare's fault" and "Darn it, Clare." Whatever. I'm going in. Someone has to.

Chapter Five
Her Kinda Crazy

Zoe

If Clare seriously thinks I'm going to listen to her, she's more nuts than Host. She's known me for what? Three decades now? She should know I'm not giving away our one shot at true love! Ten more minutes of this stupid group and I get to see him. Ten minutes. I can do this.

"…do you?"

Great. What did I miss. Why are they all staring at me? Darn it, Clare. Distracting. Always distracting.

"Do I what?"

"Are you with us, Lola?" Ann leans forward on her chair into the group. It occurs to Zoe that she's leaning so far she might actually fall off.

"Yes. I'm fine. I just didn't hear you. No one can hear anything over Tina's constant bubble blowing."

"Really? Really? 'Cause I'm not even chewing gum today," Tina retorts, glaring at her former roommate.

Zoe looks at the floor and mumbles, "Sorry."

"I'm a little worried about you. You seem distant today, Lola. Have you had time to see the psychiatrist?"

"Had time? All I have is time. And it's not like I have much control over who I do and don't see," Zoe says, glancing at the clock above Ann's head, which tells her she has exactly seven minutes to kill before she can escape what is beginning to feel like an inquisition. *Why can't they just leave me alone? I need to get ready to see Dr. Ross.*

***

"Look, ya'll. I'm telling you, and you don't have to believe me, but don't blame me when I'm right, Zoe is determined. You need to stop fighting and call a truce. Now. Is everyone here? Maria, did you do a head count?"

"Everyone's here. I don't get why Zoe would do that. Host has been practically catatonic," Maria says, questioning the wildest alter, who somehow looks older.

"No, Maria. You haven't been paying attention. She's been attending groups, making friends, stealing crap again. I don't think poor Edna will ever find her lipstick."

"Are you sure?"

"Yes, I'm sure! Why won't you guys listen and believe me?"

"You don't have a great track record," Tim points out.

"Gee. Thanks. Fine. Don't believe me. Ya'll are gonna regret this. Just watch."

"I believe you," Roy says, ignoring Tim's evil eye.

Maria jumps up, bumping into Rabbit, who yawns.

"Guys? Has it occurred to *anyone* that if Zoe is functioning and really in charge, then where is Host?"

The pons goes silent.

"Check the frontal lobe."

"Check everywhere," Roy says. "See? This is what I mean. We have to pay attention and work together. Check everywhere. She has to be in here somewhere."

Alters scurry, all of them calling for Host. But there's no answer.

Chapter Six
Father Figure

"This may sound strange to you, but I've been doing some research," Dr. Ross looks at Lola before continuing. "You know how your mother called you Dragonfly?"

Lola nods, glad the doctor is seeing her at all, but unsure of what a silly nickname has to do with anything. She can still barely make sense of why she's back at Rosewood and how Zoe convinced the doctor to see her after rumors that their relationship was going too far. *So stupid. I can't be the only one he's ever gone to a funeral with. And Zoe. Where did she go? Wasn't she just here? Why is this so confusing?*

"Well, in some cultures, people believe in totem spirit animals. My daughter's been studying it."

"Yeah, tell me about it. I know all about it. My mother was into that stuff."

"Did she ever tell you about dragonflies, specifically?"

"Probably. I think I tuned her out."

"Well, would you mind if I told you about them? Could you humor me? I think your mother may have been onto something. This could be helpful to you."

Lola isn't sure whether it's guilt or missing Stella in general that makes her agree to hear Dr. Ross out. *Maybe, it's just how handsome he is,* she concludes. *It doesn't matter why. You sound like Zoe. Knock it off.*

Dr. Ross grins at Lola, puts on his reading glasses and begins to read:

"Dragonfly spirit animals," he pauses, and continues, "...the dragonfly totem carries the wisdom of transformation and adaptability in life. As a spirit animal, the dragonfly is connected to the symbolism of change and light. When the dragonfly shows up in your life, it may remind you to bring a bit more lightness and joy into your life. Those who have this animal as totem may be inclined to delve deep into their emotions and shine their true colors."

"So? That could be for anyone," Lola can't keep listening and isn't sure why. *Just shut up! Shut up! I need to be able to think! I need to be left alone! Where did Zoe go? Where are the others? What is that weird voice? Is there another one?*

"Stick with me, okay?"

"Fine. Go ahead."

"The dragonfly is generally associated with the symbolic meaning of transformation. Dragonflies start to grow in water and then move into the air and fly.

When this spirit animal shows up in your life you may be called to transform and evolve. Symbol of metamorphosis and transformation, it inspires those who have it as a totem to bring about the changes needed in their lives in order to go to reach their full potential. When this spirit animal shows up in your life, it's an indication that it's time for change. Just like the dragonfly changes colors as it matures, you may be called to live and experience yourself differently. Stay open to the enfoldment of your personal journey." Dr. Ross looks up from his reading, grinning.

"Are you kidding? You are saying because my mother thought this was my totem animal, that I'm supposed to feel good about experiencing my life as eight different people? I'm supposed to, what was it? 'Stay open to the enfoldment of my personal journey'? Be serious!"

"No, but I *do* think it's a great metaphor. There's more."

"I don't think I can listen to more. You are starting to sound exactly like my mother. I miss her. I really do. But there were parts of her I can live without, thanks," Lola says, shifting and fighting off the urge to run out of the room. She scratches her head and bites the insides of her mouth, hoping he won't notice. She realizes the risk he's taking in seeing her again. She tells herself to be thankful. *Zoe is right, he's a good man and really does care about the system. But shut up! Please!*

If he *does* notice her indifference toward the topic at hand, Lola can't tell. He keeps reading and reading and reading.

"The dragonfly is characterized by amazing flight patterns as it appears to be able to change direction swiftly, gliding through the air with no apparent effort. Its lightness inspires those who have the dragonfly as totem to use their ability to be flexible and highly adaptable in any situation.

You can call on the dragonfly power animal when you're stuck in a situation and need assistance to gain a new perspective. The solution might lay in your ability to adapt and tackle the issue from a different angle."

Lola's mind begins to drift to other, more important things, like how to change the topic and if ever leaving Rosewood is a good idea as the doctor continues.

"…Those who have the dragonfly as a spirit animal may be encouraged to show their true colors more often and shine. Even if they may be more discreet than, let's say, the peacock, they often exert a fascinating influence and arouse curiosity in others.

When the dragonfly shows up in your life, it's perhaps time to look through illusion. A situation or someone's intentions are not clear and may be deceiving."

"Dr. Ross? Are you reading this for you or for me?" His cheeks redden and Lola laughs out loud. She decides she may be onto something here, she decides. "Well, what's your spirit animal, doctor?" Lola flips her hair and smiles at him, wide-eyed for the first time in months. "Well?"

Dr. Ross looks down at the floor and shrugs. "You know, Ms. Murray. That's a great question. Let me get back to you on that. He takes off his reading glasses and studies Lola as she squirms on his couch. "Okay. I get it. …So you don't want to talk dragonflies. What *would* you like to talk about today instead?"

Finally. "I'm so glad you asked," Lola says. "A better question might be, what *don't* I want to talk about today? My mother, my father, how to handle my step-father and why you are even bothering to see me when people think there's something going on with us, for starters."

Dr. Ross fiddles with his reading glasses and sighs. He looks at his client and finally says, "Well, alright then. Let's get to work."

"I was hoping you would say that," Lola says, surprised at the change of tone in her voice. She feels, sounds, almost, flirty. Almost.

"How are you doing about your mom?"

Lola shrugs, unsure how to answer. "Some days are better than others, I guess."

"It's really hard. ...I've been there. It takes time."

"Yeah."

"How can I help you with this? What do you need?"

"Well, you already *have* helped me. And thanks for going to the funeral with me. I can't remember if I thanked you or not."

"Only a million times," Dr. Ross says, smiling. Lola can't help but notice his perfect teeth.

"I hate that it got you in trouble."

"It's not trouble, really. People just thought we were spending too much time together. Extra sessions, me attending the funeral with you. The check up visits after. It'll be fine. You have enough to worry about. Don't worry about me. I'm thinking of retiring early, soon, anyway. I just want to get my girls through college first."

"You can't leave!" Lola clutches her chest. *Everyone always leaves! The only ones who stay are the alters, and they are like fleas!*

"Oh, no, don't worry. Nothing too soon. I'm not going to leave you. I promise."

"I can't do this without you."

"Yes, Lola, you can. I promise. But you don't have to. I'm here. I'll help you. It just can't be me. I can't help you, officially, I mean. Dr. Pezanowski is your doctor of record now, well, once the paperwork goes through."

Lola can't figure out if the grin on his face indicates sincerity or amusement. She decides not to bother trying. It's not her job to figure *him* out. It's supposed to work the other way around--"doctor of record" or not.

"Thank you. You don't know how important that is to me."

"I do know. I care about you, Lola. I won't abandon you."

"Thanks."

"You are welcome."

Lola is nearly breathless but can't figure out why. She hasn't been able to stop her mind from racing in days. *That must be it,* she decides. "That brings me to the point. My father. I can't stop thinking about him lately. My biological one. I mean, with Mom gone, I feel like an orphan and something is just, well, nagging at me. I can't explain it. I want to know more about him and I can't ask Mom now."

"That's not unusual. It makes total sense to me. I've heard this many times before.

Some clients find it helpful to get their thoughts on paper."

"You mean like a list?"

"No, I was thinking more of in the style of a letter. What if you wrote your father a letter asking him all the questions you want answers to? You wouldn't have to send it, but could."

"Hmmm. That's interesting. I guess I could try. Maybe Mom too. I feel like there's so much I never got to say. I lost so much darn time in here. I hate that I'm back here. I don't want to lose time like this anymore."

"I can imagine it's frustrating. It strikes me that you haven't brought up any of the alters. What's going on inside that head of yours? How are *they* handling all of this?"

"I refuse to talk about them. I want to do this *my* way this time. They've had *more* than enough chances. Talking about them only gives them power. Right now, I need to make this about me and me alone."

"I understand. I'm the one who was for a merge, remember?"

"I sure do."

"I'm really sorry, Lola."

"For what?"

"For everything. Just everything. It's got to be so hard."

"Yeah. Me too. Hey, Doc, what do you think my father's totem animal is?"

"You want a serious answer, or is that a joke?"

"Either, or. Do it like that word association game we play in group sometimes."

Dr. Ross chuckles. "Well, the first thought that comes to mind is missing in action. So, maybe the fox?"

"The fox?"

"Yes. They can vanish quickly and know how to hide."

"Wow," Lola laughs, "Don't hold back."

"Well, you told me to be honest."

"Fair enough. Now, do you!"

"Tiger."

"Why?"

"That topic is for another time." He grins and Lola is almost certain his cheeks are as red as hers must be.

"Yes, sir," Lola says, saluting. She twirls her hair and smiles. "*This* dragonfly needs to get ready for group anyway. Pray for me."

Dr. Ross smiles back and peers at her, "I always do."

Chapter Seven
Meeting Roy

"I cannot *believe* you guys dragged me back in here. I was doing fine. Look! I found Host and I even got her an appointment with Dr. Ross! I did that all by myself while you idiots fought over who was in charge!"

Zoe is livid. She doesn't know what to do first. It's a waste of time, she decides, to try to reason with the other alters. However, she has to convince them to let her be or her next turn won't be long enough to win Dr. Ross's heart. *All that time! And Host gets to meet with him? Really? That was my chance. Our chance! Host doesn't know how to handle a man! Host doesn't read* Cosmo!

"I think you did great, Zoe," Roy says, as Clare rolls her eyes. "Really, I do. Thank you. From all of us."

"Well, finally! A man with some common sense! That will be a nice change around here!" Zoe is still yelling. Her screech is so loud that it wakes Sam up from her nap. It takes ten minutes for Maria to get her settled in with a Peter Pan story before the alters can continue their "adults-only" meeting.

When she returns, she has only one thing on her mind.

"We have to figure out how to help Host. That halter doctor…"

"Dr. Ross. His name is Dr. Ross," Zoe interrupts.

"Zoe, I don't care what his name is. That doctor just gave Host an assignment that could set her back years. She can't handle learning about her father. Not now. She's not even over Stella yet," Maria says.

"But that's where I come in. I saw this coming," Roy says. "You had to know she'd want some sort of relationship with Henry when Stella died. I mean, it's only natural."

"Henry? I thought his name was…"

"Henry is the alter Stella fell in love with. Henry is Host's father. Who cares what the host's name was."

"Host's father had DID?" Clare's mouth hangs open. "How many were there?"

"Too many. And it's a story for another time," Tim says, finally aligned with Roy and Maria. "We need to focus here. Maria is right, Host is heading for trouble. She's barely back with us. We can't mess this up. She can't afford many more breaks like that. I mean it."

"Do you really think I'm here to cause trouble? I'm the one who tried to warn you guys about Zoe."

"There was nothing to warn anyone about! I was doing fine, right Roy?" Zoe bats her eye lashes, hoping her charm will help keep the newest alter on her side.

"Right, Zoe," Roy says, smiling wide.

"Oh, please!" Clare says. "This is like being the fifth wheel on a double date. I'm out of here. Let me know what you guys come up with. This is a waste of my time. I have a set to write."

Clare doesn't bother to wait around for them to beg her to stay—something they don't do anyway. Instead, she decides they can handle it without her. *That's what they do.*

"I have an idea. A compromise," Roy says. "Hear me out. Okay?"

"Fine! We don't have a lot of time," Maria says. "And we can't let Host hear us."

"Zoe did do a good job. She really did. Host is back with us and that's the most important thing. I suggest we let Zoe take charge as the main personality again and bring Host in with us. Then, we have Maria introduce me to her, officially. She *has* to know something is off. Clare told me that even as the main, you can hear rumblings. She must be confused."

"Why Zoe? She's going to cause trouble for Dr. Ross?"

"No I'm not!"

"Zoe! Be quiet; let Tim talk."

"Fine. I'm out of here, too. Let me know when you need me. And thanks, Roy," Zoe says.

"No, Zoe, stay. We need you."

Zoe smiles. *He needs me.* "Okay."

"Thank you."

"But keep your mouth shut," Tim adds.

"Fine." Zoe moves next to Roy.

"So anyway, we need to generally introduce me to Host. It will only confuse her more if we don't do it immediately. That, alone, could cause her to dissociate or take on another alter. We don't need more alters."

Tim grunts.

Roy continues, "She trusts you the most Maria. You need to reassure her that it's going to be okay. That I'm okay. That I'm one of you."

"Lovely. Okay. I guess we can try..."

"Yes!" Zoe shouts. "Roy! You're the best!"

"Zoe, behave!" Tim and Maria say in unison.

***

"I don't understand. You're telling me that you've been with us all along? Why haven't I known about you?" Lola asks.

"Maria, explain this, please. It makes no sense."

"What he's trying to say is that he's been there, like you said, all along, for you. For all of us, really. He feels bad that you didn't have a father, and so he felt like he should be there but not get too involved. He knew this day would come where you would need a father figure, and he's here for you now," Maria says.

"I have a real father. With Mom gone, I can reach out to him. Dr. Ross wants me to write him a letter. And I'm not even sure if I want to. I don't understand the point. Why wouldn't you *say* something? Tim was here. He was a father to me, sort of," Lola says.

"See?" Tim smiles. "And thanks, Host."

"Look, I'm not trying to take away anything from anyone. Everyone had their own roles. I was here first and I thought the best way to protect you was to keep my mouth shut. I knew it wouldn't be easy living with other people inside you. I thought I was doing the right thing. I'm starting to think I might have been wrong," Roy says. "What I *do* know, is that I'm sorry your father couldn't be there for you, Host. I'm sorry that he wasn't there to …"

Lola squeezes her eyes shut. Memories of her college rape come racing through her mind. They are so vivid, she's sure the others can see them. She's mortified.

"Where's Sam?"

"She's with Clare. Don't worry," Maria says.

"Okay, thanks." Lola begins to sob. "He wasn't there. He really wasn't there. I had nobody. I needed a dad. I mean, I know I had you guys. But it made me feel crazy. It still does. Everyone told me I was only making you up. They called you imaginary friends."

Roy nods. "I understand. I remember. And I'm so sorry."

"And you're telling me he was crazy too? You're saying the only thing my father ever gave me was some shitty gene to make me nuts? Is that what you're saying, guys?"

Roy begins to speak, but Maria stops him.

"We're saying that it all makes sense. We're saying that your father would have been there for you if he *could* have been. But he couldn't be. He was an alter, not a host. And, when he got help and his personalities merged, well, he just wasn't him anymore. In a way, it's a good thing. He never left you. He just couldn't be there for you. He wanted to be. Think of it that way, Host."

Lola's mind races. The reality of a merge and what it would mean to so many people—people outside of her—is too much to think about. *I may be nuts, but I'm not mean. I don't want to hurt people. Even the alters. This is just too much. I'm only one person!*

"I'm not sending him that letter. I'm not doing it. I need to do what the shrinks tell me to do. I need to bless the past and move forward. And there's no way we can merge."

"Well, I don't know about that, Host. I think a merge is up to you," Roy says.

"Where's Zoe? She's going to do it to Dr. Ross! She'll do what my father did to my mother. We have to stop her. He'll fall in love with her and if there's a merge, he'll get hurt," Lola says. "He's a great guy. He really cares. He spent like three days researching stupid dragonflies just to try to help me. We have to stop her."

"Host, stay calm. Zoe promised she would be good. It's going to be okay. We'll work something out. We always do," Maria said.

"We do? Because it seems like we are exactly where we started--in a nut house! We have to get out of there."

"Finally!" Tim says. "Finally. It's what we've been trying to tell you all along."

Chapter Eight
Leaving Rosewood 2.0

One month later…

Lola

I'm not sure how I feel about going to live with Charlotte when I get out of here. As kids, we were pretty close. It happens when two only children the same age get slammed together in a blended family. At the same time, people change. Boy, do I know it! I have no real memories of my step-sister since my college days. I don't know her as an adult. But what choice do I have, really?

I'd feel awkward asking Travis to let me come home. I'm sure he'd let me. He's always treated me like his own daughter. But he's another one I don't have many memories of. The thing with being nuts— my kind of crazy—is that you forget things a lot. You have a hard time separating reality from the voices and people in your head. I know Travis is a good guy. But he's Mom's guy. And she's gone. He needs time to grieve her, like we all do.

Dr. Ross and I have been working hard on figuring this all out. He says I need to get out of Rosewood sooner, rather than later. Zoe, of course, is convinced it's because he's in love with us. I have to admit; I wish that was true. She and I have been taking turns. He doesn't seem to mind or know the difference.

I tell myself it wouldn't work anyway. He has his own life, and I have no life at all. Or, I have nine. I can't figure that out either. But we do talk a lot, and Maria says it's good practice for learning how to get to know people. It's not normal to only know how to make friends in support groups where a therapist is forcing you to. Maria thinks it will be important for me to make new social connections, apart from Rosewood or family, when I'm finally on the outside.

With Roy around, I think about my birth father often. He may be connection number one. Some days, I'm tempted to reach out to him when I get out of here. Still, I'm so mad at him. I want to ask him about his own merge though. I wonder if he remembers it or if he regrets it. I wonder if he's happier now. I know he was, for a little while, when he had that other family. And sometimes, I wonder, if he ever *truly* merged. He was calling Mom a lot. Was that him or his alter, Henry?

It would be good to know someone who understands what it's like to have DID. But I'm afraid what I might find out and what the alters might think. They have been good to me. And the reality is that I've had several father figures along the way – Tim, Roy, Travis, even Dr. Ross in a funny sort of way. What right do I have to complain or ask for more?

I only have a week to figure this all out. They are moving me into a partial hospital hospitalization program as soon as I get my release plan set up. Basically, once I get everything signed off and my medication schedule, I'm out of here. It's terrifying and exciting, too.

I'm not sure if I'll go back to school. Dr. Ross suggested a writing group. I may take him up on that. I like spending time with him, and he said the group is so quirky and fun it will feel like group therapy – something I'm all too used to. I need this time to be different. I can't go back again. It's now or never. Last time I had a shot outside of Rosewood, I did things too fast and took on too much. These are the things I've learned with Ann and the rest of the group. At least I won't have to miss them.

I'm getting ahead of myself. The recovery patients have a saying: "One day at a time." That's how I need to handle this, too. Today is an exciting one. First, I have Charlotte and Travis coming for visits. I'm excited to see them both. I don't remember much of the funeral or visits from them afterwards. It might be hard to face them, so I've written everything I want to say down. Dr. Ross taught me that too.

***

"I'm not sure why you would feel uncomfortable. We're here for you. We'll make it as comfortable as we can. I promise!"

Lola wishes she could hug Charlotte. She wishes she hadn't told her she's nervous about going to live with her and her family. It's not Charlotte's fault that she's been away so long. "It's not you! I hope you get that. It's just that things have changed. You have a family now. They don't need me hanging around. I should have a life of my own, like you."

"But you *do* have a life of your own! And everyone loves you! The kids are excited about this. It will be fun. And, I could use your help. I'm like a taxi cab driver these days. It's always somewhere. Lessons, practices. It's nonstop. You could really help us out."

"Really?"

"Really! The older the kids get, the more work it is. No one warns you about that. I always thought them being babies and totally dependent would be the hard part. I was wrong. And besides, I've really missed you."

"Okay. This will be good. I'm not sure I'm going back to school right away. I wanted to get back so I wouldn't lose the classes and credits I'd earned. Obviously, it's too late for that. Dr. Ross thinks I should try to take it a little slower this time."

"Dr. Ross? Oh. Are you still seeing him? I thought you had a new therapist now?"

"Yes. I see him. He's really not bad, Charlotte. He's on my side."

"A little too much on your side if you ask me."

"It's not like that, I promise. Please, don't cause any more trouble for him. He's a good man, and he's helping me."

"If you say so. Just be careful. Mom's not around. I have to try to look out for you. It's my job," Charlotte says, tapping Lola's knee. "I wasn't causing trouble for him. I was just worried about you."

"I'm old enough to take care of myself. I know what I'm doing, and he isn't doing anything inappropriate. He just likes me and cares about me and what happens to me."

"Okay. I trust you. I'm just happy you are back. It was scary for a while there. I was worried you were going to totally leave us again," Charlotte says. "What's it like when you leave?"

Lola shrugs. "Most of it, I can't remember. Other times, I can but it's not something that's usually pleasant. This disease is hard."

"I can't imagine."

"What's worse is I'm not sure I'd want it any other way. I'm so used to it that I don't know who I would be *without* DID."

"It sounds like a bad relationship."

Lola laughs. Charlotte always has a way of simplifying things. Her work as a domestic violence counselor never really leaves. "Well, sort of. Only, the alters try to help me."

"Good. I'm glad. I always worry that you're lonely."

"It's pretty impossible to get lonely as long as they are around," Lola says, smiling. She looks at her sneakers--purple Nikes Charlotte helped her pick out the last time she was out of Rosewood. "I do worry how it will feel when they leave."

"When they leave? I don't understand."

"Dr. Ross and some of the alters want to merge."

"What's that?"

"When alter personalities all come together, it's called a merge. Basically, we all merge into the same dominant personality and that's who I become. So there's only one of us. The way it is for you and most people."

Charlotte's mouth hangs open. Her forehead creases before she finally speaks. "They can *do* that? I mean, they know *how* to do that? ...Why haven't they done that before?"

"Well, it's not a guarantee. It takes a lot of therapy and medications and the alters have to cooperate," Lola says. "More important, I have to cooperate."

"Well, why wouldn't you? That seems so much easier."

"For starters, I'm worried about who I'd even be. I don't know what it's like to live without them, Charlotte. It's like throwing away family," Lola brushes tears from her eyes as Charlotte reaches to hug her.

***

"How have you been? We've been worried about you."

"I'm more worried about how *you* have been. I'm so sorry I freaked out and haven't been there for you guys. I'm sure it's so hard for you without Mom," Lola says, hoping her step-father can see her sincerity. While she's never been able to truly accept him as a parent, it hasn't been lost on her that he's always been kind to her and Stella. All this talk of fathers lately has had her missing Travis more than she'd expected she would.

"I'm okay. It's hard."

Lola nods, wishing she knew what to say. So many years at Rosewood have left her feeling disconnected from her family, but not indifferent. She presses her lips together and looks at the floor. *I should have let Zoe stay in charge.*

"I'm sorry I didn't come see you sooner. I've been trying to work through that stuff. Your mother left a lot undone and I'm trying to figure out where things are."

Lola looks up at her step-dad and laughs. "Yeah, Mom wasn't exactly organized."

"You can say that again. I still have no idea where the checkbook is. Found one from 1985, but nothing current."

"Yep. That's Mom. She liked to hang on to everything. But never could find the one thing she needed," Lola says. And then: "I miss her."

"We all do."

"I didn't get to say goodbye. I wasted half my life in here and never got to say the things I should have said," Lola says.

"Lola, she knew."

Lola shakes her head from side to side. "No, I always gave her shit for being so flakey. I always criticized her and told her to leave me alone. She drove me nuts and she knew it. I feel horrible. It didn't mean I didn't love her."

"She knew."

"All those letters she wrote me and I never wrote back. I didn't even know about them. Maria hid them from me. She thought they would hurt me."

"Maria?"

"Oh. Yes. One of my "imaginary friends" – alters."

"Oh."

"Well, it's not too late. Write her letters back now. She'll get them. I hear they get mail in heaven."

Lola stares at the aging man, the closest thing she's ever had to a real father, for the first time in years. In him, she sees a combination of Dr. Ross, Roy, and the biological father she's imagined in her mind. "Write a letter? That's what Dr. Ross said."

"Smart man. Keep him around." Travis winks.

Chapter Nine
Table for Two

"Thanks for sticking up for me. Maria and Tim can be hard to deal with. They always think they have the answers and that Clare and I are clueless," Zoe says, wishing Roy had made his presence known years ago.

"Ha! You think?" Roy laughs, glad to be alone with Zoe for the first time. For years, he's watched her fight the other alters for a shot at true love. He finds it endearing. It reminds him of Stella in her younger years – when she first met Travis.

"It's true! I mean, look at them! They tell me I'm wrong for wanting to see if Dr. Ross' feelings for Host are real, all while denying feelings for each other. They've been like an old married couple for years and couldn't even see it for themselves. How pathetic! When love's staring you in the face, how can you be so blind?"

"I don't know. I think there's that whole complication of being alters," Roy says, watching Zoe's face wrinkle. "Oh, don't pout! I'm just saying."

"No, I'm serious. I'm right and you know it. Alters-smalters. Who cares. Love is love in any form."

"Maybe Tim was afraid he wouldn't be able to escape her if things went bad. Halters can't move to another zip code. Those two are sort of stuck in here together. Maybe he thought it would be too complicated."

"You sound like Host and her whole thing about normies. Do you remember that? How much have you missed?"

"I've been around for it all. I haven't missed a thing."

Zoe looks up. "Nothing?"

Roy smiles, "Nope."

"How do you *do* that? I could *never* stay quiet all that time. A whole lifetime!"

"You're a chick."

"Wow. You sound like Tim. Are you sure you aren't twins?"

"Oh, come on. Lighten up. It was funny."

"Yeah. It was."

"So, what do you think about this whole Dr. Ross thing? I mean, Host is probably screwing everything up. But if she isn't…"

"What do I think? What do you mean?" Roy gulps, wondering how to handle his favorite alter's question.

"Do you think I—we—have a chance with him?"

"Well, a better question might be do 'we' even want a chance with him? I don't know about the others, but I don't!"

"Oh, come on Roy. I don't mean it like that. You know what I mean. And, like it or not, Host is a woman. It's not my fault that you got stuck in here—in all of this. She deserves a life too."

"Yeah. Remember that."

"What do you mean?"

"Nothing."

"Oh, come on, tell me. You know I hate secrets. Surprises are the worst unless you're the one giving them."

"I just remember a conversation between you and Maria. You guys were talking about the merge. You asked her why anyone would ever want one. She told you that Host deserves a life, too—she gave up hers for us."

"That's so unfair and so untrue. I remember that. Nobody ever thinks about how we didn't get a choice. Somebody screwed up. We didn't get our own host bodies. It's not our fault. Why should we pay for that?"

"I don't think any of this is really about fault. I think it just is what it is."

"Now you sound like Frog. You really are such a guy." Zoe giggles.

"That's what the rumor is."

"There are a lot of rumors about you. It's scandalous."

"Really? What kind?"

"For starters, Clare doesn't think you've been here all along. Frog and Rabbit either. They think you just showed up when Stella died."

Roy shrugs. "To each his own. At least it will give Frog something to contemplate. He's been sort of out of it."

"He didn't have a good experience on the outside. I think he's given up. Rabbit's the same. But she's Rabbit. I'm surprised she hasn't killed us all off yet."

"Ssssh. Be careful. You never know who is listening, and we don't want to give anyone any ideas. The last thing we need is her cutting again. We'll never make it out of Rosewood."

"Yeah. Well, if I could get to Dr. Ross, we'd be out of there in no time. Look how far I got with him. We're practically out!"

"I know. You did good. I'm proud of you."

Zoe blushes. "You are?"

"Of course."

"Thanks!"

"You're welcome."

"Hey Roy?"

"Yeah."

"Do you wanna hang out today? I mean, I have nothing to do…"

"Sure. I'd love that."

Zoe melts.

***

"Are you hearing this?"

"How could I not?"

"Do you think it's okay?"

"Maria! You have to stop worrying so much. You're going to kill us all. If Roy and Zoe want to hang out, let them! What's it going to hurt? At least he'll be distracted and can stop telling everyone what to do. …Mr. Know-it-all… I'm so sick of his shit!"

"I know but… You know how Zoe is."

"Look, it's better Roy than Dr. Ross! And this way Host can focus on getting better and getting us out of that place."

"True."

"If you want to worry, worry about Frog, Rabbit, Clare and Sam."

"Why? What's wrong with them?"

Tim sighs, unable to comprehend why Maria's been so distracted lately: It's so unlike her. "For starters, they are isolating. Haven't you noticed how quiet it's been around here?"

"Well, no. Not really. You've been fighting with Roy. That's all I hear."

"Well listen more closely."

"It never ends! God, I feel horrible. I'm going to go find Sam. You're right. No one's paid any attention to her. I'll go do something with her now."

"Yeah, I'm coming with you."

"Good. Bring Peter Pan."

"God. I'm so sick of that guy."

"Me, too!"

Chapter Ten
Second Chances

One week later…

Lola can hardly believe she's out. She looks around Charlotte's immaculate beige kitchen, wondering what she should do first. The alters have been unusually quiet, which is probably a good thing. *Clare would have a field day with this kitchen. The first thing she'd want to do is paint it red.*

"Coffee?" Charlotte asks, reaching for a K-cup.

Lola shakes her head. "It feels like so long ago since I was out of there. And, really, it's not. Your place is just so different than Mom's."

"Well, yeah. Mom's was familiar. I mean, all Mom's stuff. That woman never could throw anything away." Charlotte laughs.

"When did you start calling her mom?" Lola asks, wishing she could take it back the second the question leaves her lips.

Charlotte's smile fades.

"I'm sorry. I didn't mean that how it sounded," Lola says. "I mean, I think it's great that you called her that and I'm sure it made her feel good and all that…"

Charlotte puts the K-cup on the counter and joins Lola at the kitchen table. Sitting across from her, she smiles at her step-sister before speaking.

"You know; I really don't know. I guess I never really thought about it. It must have just happened over time."

"I only asked because I never called Travis Dad."

"Oh! That makes sense. Well, I doubt he cares. He's a guy. He knows you love him. Women are more worried about stuff like that."

"Yeah. I guess. I've just been thinking a lot about my own father. It made me think of Travis, and then you and Mom. Everything is so complicated. I heard that my father had some, well, issues."

"Issues?"

"I heard he had DID too."

"Oh. Wow. Gosh, Dr. Ross really needs to keep his mouth shut."

Lola isn't sure whether or not to correct her sister. *Would it be worse for her to think Dr. Ross is a jerk—which she already thinks anyway—or that I'm talking that clearly to my alters again?* "I guess I just don't know what to do with that information. I mean, in a way it's good to know. In other ways, it scares me."

"But DID isn't hereditary, right? I mean, they say it comes from trauma."

Lola shakes her head. "I thought the same exact thing. But they've done new studies and it does seem just a little too coincidental to me…"

"I hear ya. I'd feel that way, too."

"I was thinking about contacting him."

"Really?"

"Well, I probably won't. It was just a thought. There's a part of me that wants to know why he left us and how DID has impacted his choices. I guess I want to believe that that's why he left, that it wasn't me."

"Oh you can't think it was you! Weren't you a baby?"

"I was like one."

"Lola, be serious. How could it possibly be your fault? You have to stop doing this to yourself! Have you told Dr. Ross this?"

"No. Well, sort of."

"Well talk to him about this again. That's the silliest thing I have ever heard. And I know Dad would love it if you called him Dad. I mean, if that's what you want."

"I don't know what I want anymore. I'm just glad to be home."

"I'm glad you're home, too. We've missed you."

***

Lola steps out of Dr. Ross's car. She can't figure out what stings more, the brisk air hitting her face, or the concept that she has no memory at all of being at the cemetery before. She makes a mental note to ask the alters if someone else was the main personality at her mother's funeral. *How could I block this? Am I really that weak?*

"Are you okay?"

"Yes. I'll be okay. Which one is hers?"

Dr. Ross points to a modest granite stone at the base of a hill. "That one."

Together, they walk toward Stella's grave. The headstone reads: "Stella Renee Murray-Kingston. Wife. Mother. Friend." It lists her birth and death dates and has a small monogram of Stella's initials. But what catches Lola's eye is the tiny dragonfly etched above the word mother. She gasps.

"Lola, if it's too much we can go back to the car. I know this is hard for you."

Silence.

Lola takes her glove off and stuffs it in her coat pocket. She runs her fingers over the headstone and traces the dragonfly. A tear—frozen by winter's grasp--sticks to her cheek.

"I don't even know what to say. Or think." *Where is Maria? I need Maria.*

"It's okay. It's understandable."

"I don't know what to do."

Dr. Ross stretches his arms open, inviting her in for a hug. She finds herself in his arms, clinging to him and crying.

"I can't be here. I have to go."

"Then let's go. We can go back to my office. I can take you home. We could go get some hot chocolate. Whatever helps you. I knew it might be too soon. I shouldn't have taken you here."

"I asked you to."

"I should have known better."

They walk back to his car in silence. Lola swallows the guilt of not staying longer and promises herself she'll come back when it's easier. The last thing Stella would want is her going crazy again. *You have to stay strong. You can't let this get to you.*

They drive in silence for a few minutes before Dr. Ross asks Lola where she wants to go.

"Honestly, I really don't know. I just like driving around."

"Okay, then, me too."

They drive random miles, talking about anything, but Stella. For Lola, it's comforting. Still, she can't help but wonder where the alters are. Normally, they all rush to the frontal lobe the minute they sense her being upset. She knows she shouldn't, but is tempted to call for them. Instead, she reminds herself to be strong.

"...book club. It's really a great group. So it's not all writing. There's reading too. It's honestly more like a support group. We try to convince each other not to give up."

Lola has to take a few minutes to catch up. She realizes he's talking about his writing group, which meets weekly at the library. It's the one thing he does for fun, she's discovered in the months of working with him both on and off the record.

"It sounds like my group stuff with the PHP. It's funny. I actually look *forward* to it now. I missed them all the first time I was out, and I'm sure I will again. I like that I can stay connected to Rosewood with group."

"You can never have enough support. And it is a lot like that. I'm constantly thinking of quitting. But it's the other writers who keep me going back to the pen," Dr. Ross says, pulling into a diner. "I'm hungry. Mind if we stop here for something to eat? I hear they have the best apple pies. And, honestly, I have nothing at home. I haven't done the groceries and when the girls aren't around, I am horrible about feeding myself."

"No, not at all. I love apple pie."

Three hours pass before Lola and Dr. Ross decide it's time to go.

"Charlotte's going to have a heart attack. She'll think I kidnapped you."

"Charlotte's not my mother," Lola says, climbing back into his car. "But I hope this doesn't get you in trouble."

"No. Not at all. It's called exposure therapy. And, hell, there's walking therapy. Therapy can take on all kinds of forms. Today, we faced a fear together. And you did great, by the way. That took a lot of bravery to go there. I know how terrified you were. I'm proud of you."

Lola blushes. She's thankful for the darkness in his car.

"Man, it's gotten cold."

"I know."

When they pull up in Charlotte's driveway, Lola's surprised to see that no one is home. She decides they may have gone out to dinner—something Charlotte had talked about. She can't help but feel a little left out.

"Well, thank you for bringing me home," she says, reaching for her purse off Dr. Ross's car floor.

"It was my pleasure."

"Actually, thank you for everything. I know you went out of your way to help me today. I really appreciate it."

"You're very welcome, Lola. You are important to me. I care about you."

"I bet you say that to all your clients," Lola says, surprised at how flirtatious it sounds. "I mean. I bet you are a great doctor for everyone."

Dr. Ross chuckles. "No, Lola, you are different. And, technically, as soon as that referral goes through, I'm not even your primary doctor anymore."

Lola doesn't know how to make sense of the butterflies in her stomach. She can't tell if they come from a fear that Charlotte was right and he's an unethical jerk, or the fact that she wants him to be. At the moment, she's not sure it matters.

"How?"

"How?"

"Yes. How am I different?"

"Oh, wow. Let me count the ways. You fascinate me. You always keep me on my toes. You're fun. You're young at heart. There are a million reasons. You're just so different than … never mind."

"Than who?"

"No, nothing, it was stupid. You're just unlike anyone I've ever met. You really are a dragonfly. It suits you."

The sound of her mother's nickname for her melts Lola. After a day of mixed emotion, it feels like a cherry on top of something sweet. Or, maybe even apple pie. She smiles.

"Lola, you can call me Aaron if you want. Dr. Ross just sounds so formal."

"Oh, no! I'd never."

"Really. I want you to."

"But why?"

"Well many clients do it. Really. It's no big deal, and I'd like it. It's so much more comfortable. I mean, we've been through a lot together, and I feel like part of your life."

"Okay, then. I'll try it, Aaron."

Saying his name is strange. At the same time, it does feel more natural. "Well then, I should be getting in. No clue when Charlotte and the rest of them will be home."

"Let me walk you to the door. It's pitch black out and there's ice everywhere. The last thing you need is a fall."

Lola doesn't argue. Instead, she laughs. It reminds her of how Travis would never let Stella leave the car without walking around to open her door.

At the front door, Lola fumbles for her keys. It's been months since she's used keys and it only makes her more nervous that Aaron's watching her. Finally, she asks him to help. It's then, when he reaches over to open the door, that he kisses her.

Chapter Eleven
Frog

"Host?"

"Yes, Frog?"

"Oh, good. You're up."

"I can't sleep."

"You and me both. Is everyone up?"

"No, it's just us."

"Okay, good. What's up?"

"I saw you today, with Dr. Ross."

Fabulous. "Oh."

"Don't worry, I don't see a need to tell anyone, yet. But do you know what you're doing?"

"Um. Hell no. I have no clue. But thank you for not broadcasting it."

"You're welcome."

"Are you okay?"

Frog laughs. "I have no clue either."

"What do you mean?"

"I have no idea what my purpose is at this point. I mean, everyone's distracted. I feel like Rabbit, and she's the last person I want to be like. Love her to death, but not my idea of a good time."

It's Lola's turn to laugh. "Welcome to my world. That's how I feel with the halters. Heck, even with you alters. I feel that way all the time. Where has everyone been, anyway? I wanted to talk to Maria today and she was nowhere."

"Her and Tim have been worried about Sam. And, of course, there's the new guy."

"Do you like him?"

"I wouldn't know. Zoe's laid claim to him. They haven't stopped talking all this time. I think your doctor's safe. She's found a new man."

"Wow. Just like that?"

"Come on, it's Zoe. And Roy's attainable. It makes perfect sense."

"Yeah. I guess. What does Maria think of that?"

"Who knows. No one talks to me. She's too busy worrying about Sam and Rabbit. Trying to create the perfect nuclear family or something with Tim. Probably helps her feel less guilty about how she treated your mother."

"Wow. I've missed a ton. But I bet Sam's happy."

"Oh, she's thrilled. They've even got her off of Peter Pan and on to some other kick. I can't remember what it is, but I'm sure I'll find out soon enough. Lion King maybe?"

"What about Clare? What's she been up to? I'd think she'd be ready to throw me out of here for a show or something by now."

"She's been working on a set. Nothing new there. I'm sure she'll be up to her antics in no time."

"Lovely. That ought to mess me up at just the wrong time."

"It's Clare. Is there any other way?"

"I guess not! ...Did anyone else see?"

"I don't think so. I haven't heard a word. The only one that might have is Rabbit. But she doesn't tell anyone anything. So you're fine."

"So why were you around? You never hang in the frontal lobe."

"I wanted to see if you'd let me meet with Dr. Ross."

"As the main?"

"Yes."

"Why?" *Great. He's going to threaten Aaron's life.*

"No! Nothing like that. How do you not realize I can still hear your thoughts? I'm part of you! I wanted to talk to him for *me*. This was before anything happened between you guys."

"I doubt that would be a problem at all. I see him tomorrow. I can just let him know you're coming instead. I'm not sure I'm ready to face him as myself yet anyway. You'd be doing me a favor."

"Okay. Great. On it. What time?"

"Three."

"Perfect, I'll be ready. Thanks, Host."

"You're more than welcome. It's nice to get to talk to you alone, Frog. We haven't done that in a long time."

"Yeah. It is. Thanks."

***

"I get that you're trying to help me, doc. It's just a little awkward after what happened between you and Host."

"I understand that, Frog. This is a little strange for me, too. But I can assure you that I am here to help. Lola says you wanted to speak with me."

"Yes. Thank you for seeing me."

"Any time. An alter of Lola's is always a friend of mine. How can I help you?"

"Well you know the totem animal stuff?"

"Mmm hmm."

"I hate to state the obvious, but I'm named after an amphibian. I did some research and, well, I wanted to discuss it with you. ...And, of course, there's Rabbit, too."

"Oh! Wonderful! I just love this kind of stuff."

"Yeah, me, too."

"So what did you find out?"

"Well, frogs are supposed to be great listeners and the kind of people who give great advice."

"Yes."

"But I don't feel like that's me."

"You don't?"

"No."

"I disagree!"

"How so?"

"Well frogs, as you probably know, are transformative--like dragonflies. They are adaptable and are family people. Generally, they will do whatever they need to, to make others around them happy. All of that is part of being a good listener. From everything I have heard, that is exactly you."

"I hadn't thought of that."

"It's hard to analyze ourselves sometimes. Why don't you tell me about a time you fit that description?"

"I guess there are plenty of times. Mostly, lately anyway, I try to stay out of the way. I want everyone to be happy and to be able to do their own thing. I used to think I had to get out and have a life of my own. Now, I'm not so sure. I get what you were saying, now, about a merge. It's what's best for everyone."

"So think about that. You're a young guy. Most young guys could give two shits what was going on in the system. But not you.

You are willing to make a change for the good of the larger whole. That's a frog, Frog," Dr. Ross laughs.

"Wow!"

"Neat stuff, hugh?"

"But what about Rabbit? I've never understood her."

"Rabbits are quick. They don't like being boxed in corners. Imagine what it's like being trapped in Lola's body for a person who thrives on fast movements and high energy. Rabbit has been denied those things because there hasn't been a merge. So, her natural reaction is misery. At least, that's what I think. She's a tricky one. But, they say rabbits are tricky!"

"Hmm. I hadn't thought of that either. You may be right."

"I want to get back to you for a minute, if that's okay?"

"Sure."

"Okay, give me a second," Dr. Ross turns to his laptop and quickly types in a search. He scans the screen before he speaks. "Okay, exactly what I thought. Listen to this: When the frog jumps into your life it may indicate now is a time to find opportunities in transition. It is there to help you swim easily through some tough life changes. It may also signal the need to enhance your intuition, and strengthen your connection with the spirit world. This amphibian also symbolizes coming into your own personal power."

"Wow."

"Yeah."

"So, basically, that explains why I'm okay with a merge?"

"I think you can read into it whatever you want to. But I can't say that hasn't occurred to me as well."

"I know you've always wanted the merge, but I can't really understand why. Can you explain it?"

"Well, obviously I want Lola to be happy. I honestly don't care if that includes a merge or not. But what I do see is that she has trouble trying to please everyone. I'm not sure anyone could ever please that many people. That has to be hard."

"I'm sure."

"Lately, I've been thinking, the only way to really do a merge—and make it stick—is that each of the alters needs to be happy, including Rabbit, which could be hard. Until then, I'm not sure a merge would even be possible. Lola wouldn't let it happen if she thought someone was going to suffer long term."

Frog looks at the floor. He inhales deeply. "You're right. I've tried to think about this with transcendentalism. That helps me. I know a merge is the right thing. The trouble may be convincing the others. But I think I have a plan."

"It sounds like you've got more than I do at this point. I've tried it all. Even hypnosis didn't stick. In the end, it's up to you guys. I just want her happy. Frankly, I find you all quite fun to talk to. Whatever you decide is okay by me, I assure you."

"Well, doc," Frog laughs, "I'm an insider. It helps with the whole making it stick thing."

"Ha ha. I bet it does!"

"Thanks for meeting with me. I've got work to do."

"Alrighty then. I'm glad I could help. It was nice seeing you."

"Thanks, you, too. And, doc? Treat Host good." Frog smiles and cracks his knuckles.

"Always. See you soon?"

Pop. Pop. Pop. Knuckle cracking. And then, silence.

Chapter Twelve
Clare

I don't know if Host thinks I'm dumb, or that a best friend doesn't know. I mean, seriously. How could she think I've missed all of this? Does she think Frog's the only one watching when things get quiet, ya'll? It was just a fluke that he was there. She wonders why I've been quiet? I'll tell you why.

I'm not writing a set, ya'll. I'm trying to figure out what to do. It's not easy when a girl loses her best friend; especially to a guy. I lost my two best friends in one day. Not exactly comedic material—at least not right now.

I came around the day Holly died. I don't care what my animal is. I don't believe in that crap. If I did? I'd say I was a firefly—with a broken light. She doesn't notice me anyway. I'm invisible now that she has that man. She's just as bad as Zoe. I've never been more disappointed, more betrayed.

Where was Dr. *Aaron* Ross the day her best friend died? Where was he when they took her away and threw in her a nuthouse? Not just the first time. Every single time. Was he the one making her laugh 'til she cried? I think not.

If she liked Charlotte more, maybe she'd have listened to her. Then again, I guess sisters never listen to sisters. It probably made him even more attractive to her. But let's think about this, seriously, guys.

This guy is a psychiatrist. He has an oath, a legal responsibility, not to hurt her. He's not allowed to have a relationship with her. I had Rabbit look it up. He has to wait at least two years to have a relationship with her. Even then, he has to be able to prove—in a court of law, ya'll—that he means no harm.

I'm sorry, but that's the stuff I joke about: Love and its bruises. Love hurts. It's just part of it. So how could any shrink ever say they had no intention of hurting someone? Shrinks should know better, that it always hurts.

I think he cares for her. That much is true. But he took advantage of her and there's nothing I can do to stop her. I talked to Rabbit about this. She's the only one who seems to have time for me anymore. She agrees. She says people suck and Dr. Ross is just another halter, out for himself.

If Host had come to me, I would have told her so myself. But she never came to me. She never would. And Maria says it's just because she wouldn't like my answer – that I don't understand true love. I had no ideas she was such a romantic. I don't bother with Zoe. No one's really seen her since she and Roy got together. They just sit there, giggling about things no one else can hear. It's ridiculous. Also not the stuff of comedy.

I hate this. I don't feel remotely like myself, ya'll. I want to laugh and find the humor in this, but how can I? My best friend's going to be hurt and there's nothing I can do to stop it. It's taking everything in me not to get in there—to the frontal lobe—and hit Dr. Ross.

Rabbit said the only way to know, for sure, how bad he will hurt her is to test him. So, ya'll, that's what I plan to do. *Exactly* what I plan to do. I'm just not quite sure where to start.

Of course, I could put his career on the line. But that seems too obvious and a little too mean. He is, after all, only human. And, like I said, I do think he cares about her. I could visit him directly, like Frog. Or, I could do something even trickier. That's where Rabbit comes in.

This is mean, ya'll. And you'll probably hate me. But a girl's gotta do what a girl's gotta do to protect her BFF, ya know? And Rabbit, she likes to cut. I'm thinking having Rabbit do a little creative carving might be the trick. You know, just enough to scare him. What man would stick with a woman crazy enough to make herself bleed out?

Rabbit says, if he stays, he's a keeper. She doesn't think he will. I don't either. So we can't bet on it. It will be the event of a lifetime, ya'll. I won't be able to watch. I hate watching her hurt. But it won't be Host, it'll be Rabbit. And she's into this shit. It won't take long and it will make the point: "Dude, back off."

For now, I have to play nice. When she finally does get around to telling me—if I can wait that long—I'll have to be supportive. Not too supportive. Host's not dumb. Just supportive enough. She'll never see it coming. It's a win for everyone. In the end, she's protected. Rabbit gets a release, and I get my best friend back. See?

***

"Were you *ever* going to tell me?"

"Well, of course. I just wasn't sure how."

"Did you seriously think Frog was the only one who knew? I mean, *Frog*?"

"Maybe I just wanted to believe he was the only one who knew. Did he tell you or did you see it yourself?"

"I saw. I'm not blind, ya know."

"Well, no, obviously."

"So?"

"So, what, Clare? I don't know what you're getting at."

"Well, don't you sort of have an issue with this? I mean, it's not right. I support you and all. Do what you want to do. I mean, you go girl, but still…"

"Okay, hold up. Of course I'm nervous about it. I don't exactly know what I'm doing. The closest thing I've had to being hit on by a guy in years is by Justin at Rosewood. And he's a kid! The whole thing makes me nervous. But it's nice. Aaron's good to me. It's nice to have someone to talk to."

"There are seven, eight, of us to talk to! Why do you need people to talk to? Talk to us! We haven't talked in ages!"

"It's not the same. I mean he is a human being, not a voice in my head. He makes me feel … normal. Important even."

"Important? You don't think you're important to us? For Christ sakes, Host, you are our main! Without you, we wouldn't exist! You can't get more important than that."

"Clare, you just don't understand. I love you guys, all of you. I just need some normal relationships. You don't know what it's like trying to function in the world and not knowing who you are. It's hell."

"What's hell is being unappreciated by your best friend."

"I do appreciate you! I have missed you! I've asked about you and worried about you. Frog said you were working on a set so I didn't want to bug you. I wanted to give you space to do your thing. I know, better than anyone, how that feels."

"Fine. You're right. I don't like to be bothered when I'm doing my set prep. That's true."

"Listen, Clare. I love you. I can't say that enough. I need you! You are my BFF and you and Maria are two of the biggest reasons I've always been hesitant about a full merge. I don't know what I'm doing here. I need you guys, probably more than ever. I don't want to screw this up. Aaron's a really great guy."

"It's not like I have a clue. That's something you should talk to Maria or Zoe about. At least they have some experience."

"But I don't think it's the same. They are doing this without, well, bodies for starters! I'm supposed to kiss this guy and I don't even know if I'm doing that right. I mean, I guess I am."

Clare laughs for the first time in nearly a month. "Oh, I wouldn't worry about that. You sure looked like you knew what you were doing based on his reaction."

"You think?"

"Yes, you idiot. I do."

"Okay. Good. I have been dying to ask someone, but I wasn't about to ask Frog. So I thought I was on my own."

"You never have to be on your own. Even if there's a merge, that doesn't mean we don't exist."

"A merge? I thought we dropped that? I mean, temporarily. And you? You've never been in favor of a merge."

"A girl can change her mind."

"Wait, what? You want to merge?"

"I just don't really see any point. I mean, everyone was here for a reason. Tim and Maria have each other now and don't exactly need to parent or protect you. You're getting a best friend in Dr. Ross. That counts me out. I have no idea about this stupid animal totem or totem animal crap and the purpose of Rabbit and Frog. Zoe and Roy are all tied up. Now seems like the best time ever to merge. Rabbit would be thrilled, that's for sure."

"I don't even know what to say. Are you not listening, Clare? I need you."

"Maybe that's exactly the problem. Or, maybe, when you stop needing us, a merge will be easy. Either way, something's got to give. You can't expect Tim, Frog and Roy to be okay with running into the sunset with Dr. Ross, can you?"

"No one said anything about running off into the sunset. We're just having fun. He's going to start taking me to writers' groups and help me get reenrolled in school, my own place, stuff like that."

"See? What do you need us for? I see him doing pretty much all of it."

"Oh Clare. He's never going to be you."

"Well, Host. You will never be the same with him."

Silence. And then: "Does he make you happy?"

"Yes. He makes me happier than I've ever been."

"Oh."

***

I feel like the shitty maid of honor who secretly hopes the bride trips or has a fling with the groom on rehearsal dinner night. What kind of friend am I, ya'll. I've got to get to Rabbit. I can't have her cutting my bestie. I can't have any of this. There's really only one thing we can do, which is merge. I never thought I'd hear myself saying it, but that's what a best friend would do.

I want Host to be happy. When she said he made her happy, it was literally the first decision and statement I ever heard her make on her own. She didn't check with anyone. She didn't hesitate. She just said yes. So, I know it's true. Like it or not, Host has found her one true love. Zoe might have been right all along.

Would I have picked him? Heck no. I'd have picked a cowboy, ya'll. But I don't get to pick. I'm the best friend. That's my job. And, frankly, I'm now out of a job. I'm unemployed in the BFF line of work, ya'll. Yeah, I know he'll never replace me. I never replaced Holly either. But she'll be okay. It's time for me to go. That's what a BFF would do.

I'd make a joke, but I'm not in a joking mood. I need to stop Rabbit. Then, I've gotta convince the others. It's time to merge. Gotta go...

Chapter Thirteen
Rabbit

Clare's cute. She comes up with this great plan. Says I can cut. Doesn't realize, of course, that I plan to take it a whole lot further than that. But then, just because Host's happy, Clare wants to take it all back. It doesn't work like that. You can't hire a hit man then ask for your money back. I've got it all planned out. I'm going in there, doing what Frog did, talking all that crap about why I'm a rabbit and what it means to the greater scheme of things, then I'm showing him what real crazy looks like.

I miss Frog already. The others haven't even noticed he's missing. It only makes me feel lonlier and more resolved. I mean, how bad can it be? Frog did it. I can too. I suppose I could do it his way, quietly. But I don't think the others would follow. This way, there's no choice. You can't help but merge in death, right?

I don't know when Clare became such a softie. She always had a spirit no one could touch. Lately, she just hasn't been herself. I think it's because she's lost her purpose. Host has better things to do. As for me? I don't think I ever had one. At least, not one that I could find. Maybe this is my purpose, to finish it all.

***

"It's great to see you, Rabbit. I can't remember the last time. Hypnosis maybe?"

Rabbit shrugs. "Don't know."

"Well I'm glad you're here. I talked to Frog last week and it went well. Did he tell you?"

Rabbit nods. She can't help but be curious about the pictures on his bookshelf. *Does Host know he has daughters? They must be his. That's just more drama. They look only a little older than me. What would she do with that? And who is the woman? Secret family? Host probably knows nothing. This guy is scum.*

"So how can I help you today?"

Play the game. Rabbit twists the knife in Host's sweatshirt pocket. The cold medal in her hand is so tempting she wishes she didn't have to wait.

"I wanted to hear about rabbit totem animals. I mean, that's what I'm named for. I figured I should know. Maybe it will help me figure out how to be happier or something, I don't know."

"Awesome! You came to the right guy! My daughter got me into this with a term paper. Now I'm obsessed and am even writing a novel about it."

"About totem animals?"

"Well, no, not that simple. This one is a mystery and involves a dead fish."

"A dead fish?" *Sounds interesting.*

"Silly, I know."

"Actually, I'd like to hear."

"I'm really not supposed to get into personal details. I'm supposed to help you in a professional capacity."

Rabbit smirks and raises her eyebrows. *Does he think I don't know?*

"Okay. Good point. You really want to know?"

At least the guy can take a hint. He's almost ...likeable. And he did come out and talk about his daughter. It can't be a secret family.

"Yes. Dead shit fascinates me."

"Okay then."

"Go."

"During my divorce, which wasn't pretty, I had the same dream every night. The dream was that I had a pet fish—it looked like Nemo from the movie—that I took everywhere with me. His name was Milo. The problem was I would sit him on my lap and forget to give him water. I'd only notice he was dying when he began to flap around."

Wow. He's a wacko too. They are perfect for each other. Rabbits jaw drops. "Go on," she smiles.

"So Milo and I are at this amusement park. We're on this ride where you sit in a cart, almost like a haunted house. The ride breaks. There's no water anywhere and Milo is flapping around in my lap. I panic and jump out of the cart and throw him in a puddle on the ground. Only the puddle has suction—like in a pool. He gets sucked in and all his colors, that bright orange of clown fish, bleeds into the water. From there on out, I bleed orange."

"What? That is the craziest dream I have ever heard."

"Oh, trust me, I know."

"So what did you do?"

"I had that dream every night for like a year. I looked it up online. I talked to dream readers, anything you could think of. It turns out, dreaming of a dying or dead fish symbolizes misfortune like losing money, or loss like losing a relationship." Dr. Ross laughs. "Trust me, as a guy getting divorced from a woman like my ex, you're bound to lose each."

"Damn."

"So I saw the symbolism."

"But how did you stop the dream?"

"I didn't. It wasn't until the divorce was final, and I fixed things with my wife that it happened less. Eventually, I just stopped having it."

"That's crazy."

"Not really. Not if you believe in dream interpretation and totem animals, which brings me to you."

"I don't care about me. Never have. I want to know more about the dead fish thing."

"Okay, what do you want to know?"

Rabbit takes her hands out of Host's sweatshirt. She looks at the picture behind Dr. Ross' head of his daughters.

"I'm assuming because of the fish dream, you took your daughter's totem animal assignment like ten steps further?"

"Yes. Something like that."

"Okay. Well, that changes things."

"That changes things? You lost me, Rabbit."

"Yeah. I'm a little lost too. Give me a minute."

The guy had a dream that symbolized loss of money and relationships. Obviously, getting divorced, he was losing his family relationships in the way he'd known them. And money too because it's split in half. The only way that was fixed was to fix the relationships and money. Now, make him

Host. Host made us up – well, not made up, but put us in containers. We were all part of her, like a living fish in water, until things got mixed up. Right now, we're flapping around in his lap. The way to fix that is to either 1. Go back into the water, or 2. Die. Both are great options. Back into water is a merge. Dying, well, that's cool too. At least we'd stop flapping.

"Can I tell you something?"

"Sure."

"Frog's gone."

"Frog's gone? What do you mean?"

"He merged. Simple. He, like, found water."

Dr. Ross tilts his head. He squints his eyes. "Sorry, you lost me. He found water?"

"He stopped flapping around like your fish. He like reabsorbed. He said goodbye. Not to the others. He knew they'd try to stop him. But to me. He told me his plan. He just, like, disappeared."

"Are you sure?"

"Well, doc, it's not like there's a lot of territory to cover. I've looked everywhere for him. He's really gone."

"Oh, gosh. Are you okay?"

"Am I okay? Who cares. No one ever cares if I'm okay. I haven't been okay since the beginning. Frog said that a merge didn't mean he was truly gone. He's just gone as an individual. He called in transend-something. He seemed pretty excited about it. I didn't try to stop him. People should have a choice…"

"Transcendentalism."

"Yeah, that."

"He always was a philosopher."

"Yep."

"What does Lola think of this?"

"Ha! You think Host knows? Please. She's too busy flirting with you. She has no clue. It'll take her months to find out. Everyone's too distracted. Which makes me think…"

"I'm afraid to ask. I feel horrible."

"Why would you feel horrible? You probably helped him. Besides, he has free will and he's probably happier now."

"Well, Lola for starters. She's going to be so sad! She just lost her mother. Now Frog?"

"You don't get it, do you? He's not lost! For a shrink, you really don't know your shit. You don't do ethics, and you definitely don't do your research. You do know how DID works, right? All we alters are is splits off of Host. We are all Host. Hell, the reason I'm so miserable is I'm the negative split. I would be ten times happier—whatever that is—if I was part of the larger whole. Basically, back in the water."

"I know how it works and never thought of that. I guess I don't think it's that simple. Sure, you're splits. But you're still individual. I mean, half of you have your own diagnoses too."

"Great. So we're individually nuts *and* crazy as a whole?"

"I didn't mean it like that. And I don't think *any* of you are crazy. I like you all just fine. I'm really going to miss Frog. …And I am ethical. I've referred her to another doctor. Everything will work out, you'll see. I have no intention of hurting her. I…"

"Oh, please. Just stop. You sound just like the rest of them. My ears will bleed if you keep talking like that. And it won't be orange."

What the hell am I supposed to do now? I could just disappear, like Frog, if I thought the others would follow. But then, why do I have to wait at all? He didn't. Rabbits are sneaky and quick: They do their research too. If my purpose was negativity, 'cause it can't all be sunshine and rainbows, then what is my point now? He's a good guy. She really could be happy. Just a few cuts. Nothing deep. And not in front of him. Maybe. …Or don't bother: Just peace out.

"I'm sorry. I'm not trying to make your ears or anything else bleed. You've done great with the cutting, by the way. I'm proud of you."

"Yeah. Thanks. Okay, I'm all set. I got what I needed. Thanks. You can have Host back."

"Wait, we didn't talk about rabbits!"

"It's cool. I loved the dead fish story. Thank you. Have a great day, doc."

"Host? Your man's waiting for you…"
Silence.

And, "…Coming, Rabbit."

Oh, she's going to love the knife in the pocket. Oh well. Not my problem now. I've got an ocean to explore.

Chapter Fourteen
Zoe & Roy

Zoe

I've read it in *Cosmo*, that sometimes, love is right under your nose. In my case, it was even closer. I still tease Roy for not letting us know he was here. But it's a good thing, if I'm honest.

Here's what's great about a merge: When you get married, two become one, right? Roy and I are going to get that for sure. We will be one and the same and together forever no matter what; at least as long as Host is breathing.

I'm planning a wedding before the official merge. Maria and Tim said I could. I promised I wouldn't try to stop anything. I'd just run with it if I could get that one moment. It's one I've waited all my life for. Sam will be my flower girl and Tim will marry us. I'm still debating what color to pick. I guess the cool thing about being on the inside is we can pick any color we want.

Clare says we're moving too fast. She's probably just jealous. I told her she could perform at the reception. That seemed to shut her up. She must be working on her set now. Whatever works!

It's going to be a fabulous day. I can barely contain myself. I don't know how I'll sleep, but I'll have a lifetime to sleep during the merge. I have to get going. *Cosmo* has a section on how to write your own vows. Writing has never been my strong suit.

Roy

I just want the record to show that this was never planned. Of course I loved Zoe. I've loved all of them all along. I didn't think of her in a romantic way. I mean, what would have been the point?

To me, Zoe is Host's hope. She represents everything that is pure and good in the world; which isn't a lot. She believes in true love and makes me smile. The woman can talk your ear off. But, for a guy like me, it's perfect. I don't like talking so much. I'm glad I made my presence known, for Zoe and the rest of them.

I didn't see it working out this way. It almost feels too easy. I watched poor Tim struggle for years with trying to get them to merge or escape or whatever he could think of. Poor guy. Maybe there's some truth to the idea that the way I approached this was weak. I'm not sure I know. I'm even less sure I care.

Soon, we'll all be one. Together, we will form the perfect union; giving Host back every tool she needs to live a good life. I have no idea how that will go either. I don't even know if the merge will stick. I mean, Henry was out, crying over Stella at her funeral. Or, it could have been his host body, just feeling Henry's pain because Henry had become part of him. I'd think if it were Henry himself, he'd have approached Host. She is his daughter, after all.

Host's family situation is complicated. Things always are when mental illness is involved. But it's not unlike our situation as alters. When I look at it, I see that even with her halter family, she really had it all. Travis was there for her. She already had a father in him. She didn't need Tim or me. We probably set her back, just being here. I tried to avoid that, but it was unavoidable.

I'm trying to make peace with the idea that "everything happens for a reason." This merge is meant to be. Zoe gives me hope that everything will work out for each of us, in its own way and time. I'm not sure we have any other choice.

Chapter Fifteen
Maria & Tim

Maria

I feel bad that we weren't more focused on Sam all along. Sam is Host's inner child. She's the one who needs the nurturing most of all. Instead, I was worried about Host herself. It's not like she wasn't nurtured. As much as I hate to admit it, Stella really was a good mother.

I had a conversation with Zoe a while ago, before she met Roy and got distracted. She asked me why we should give up our lives for her. I told her the answer was simple: Because she gave up hers for us. She didn't like that answer, not until she met Roy. I'm not so sure what I think of that now. I think it works both ways. We've all sacrificed for each other. And that's how a family should work.

But now it's time for Host to finally spread her wings and fly. Just because Stella's gone, it doesn't mean she's not a huge part of Host's world. I've been jealous enough about it to know it for sure. And it's taught me something. It's taught me that when you love someone, they never really forget you. You become a piece of them.

There's a saying that people come into our lives for a reason, a season, or a lifetime. We will always be part of Host's life—even with a merge. We each showed up as a split of who she is for a reason. We stayed for a season. Now, we will be with her forever. Tim says he's going to convince her that it's time for a full merge. I hope he can. It's time. I can feel it. A mother knows these things.

It will be hard. I will miss talking to her. But I have faith I won't be forgotten and that I'll be able to talk to her from time to time, through memories and her knowing me well enough to know what I'd say. The hardest part of being a mother is letting go. It's also the most important. I have to trust that she has the tools to live her own best life and set her free. It's exactly what I'm going to do.

I'm looking forward to a merge. I'm thinking of it like retirement. I won't have to be on alert all the time. I won't worry anymore. I'll be able to sit back and let things take their course. I'm sure it won't be easy at first, if I even know. I'll get used to it and adapt. I always do. It'll be worth it for Host. Now, I'm off to plan a wedding!

Tim

I spent years trying to help us escape. There was nothing I wouldn't do. I really believed there was a way out. I couldn't imagine spending the rest of my life in a woman's body. It's all I could think about. I spent all of my free time planning, plotting and scheming. I was miserable.

What I didn't see was that we didn't need a way out at all. What we needed was to embrace the moment and accept things the way they were--to make the best of the hand we were dealt. You see, we don't have to be the main personality. We weren't meant to be. Instead, we can do the things we were meant to do; serve the purposes we came here for. I was created to help protect Host. She doesn't need that anymore. She has plenty of people in her outside life who love and care for her. Inside, I've been able to help Maria nurture Sam, the little girl side of Host who got lost when this all began. By loving her, we've helped Host heal.

I can't take credit for figuring any of this out. None of us can. We got lucky, really. Or, maybe Roy was right. Maybe things just took the course they were meant to all along. Maybe a merge just couldn't happen until all the wounds were healed and Host felt safe enough to try things on her own. I feel like an idiot that I wasted all that time fighting the inevitable. But, you live and learn, I suppose.

Now, I have to help Host with all of this. I have to make her understand that we'll never really leave her—we can't. She needs to know that we've been part of her all along; not as individuals, but as actual parts of who she is. It reminds me of that saying: "United we stand, divided we fall." I need to make Host see that a merge will make her, all of us, stronger. Together, we are strong. It'll start with a mission statement. It will be our new mantra. Or one of them, anyway.

Lately, I've been worried that Roy had it right all along. If we hadn't shown up to protect her and guide her, Host still would have been okay. Instead, by interfering and making our presence known, she was never able to build confidence that she could handle life's twists and turns on her own. Now, with the merge, she'll get that. I guess it's never too late. I can't say I don't feel guilty.

Today, I'll try to rectify a wrong. I just hope she doesn't fight me. I'm too tired to fight anymore. I'm ready for a merge.

Chapter Sixteen
Sam

We're going on a great adventure. It will be like Peter Pan in Wonderland. We have no idea what it will be like or who else will be there. I'm excited. I don't know what to pack. Maria says I just need to bring a positive attitude.

I've been having so much fun with Maria and Tim and Zoe and Roy, too. They play games with me and tell me how smart I am. They think I'm the best reader ever, and I know it's true. Someday, I'm going to be a writer. I'm going to write movies about magic and superheroes. I might do a comic strip, too. In my movies, people won't die and everyone will be happy. When I grow up, I'm going to be just like Host. I'm going to break out of places I don't like and make my own rules. I can do that, you know. Tim and Roy say so! I'm so excited! Gotta go! Grand adventures are waiting for us… Oh, and I gotta try on this dumb flower girl dress. Maria said so. I wish it was blue like Tinkerbell's.

***

Lola

131

I feel like Sam; a kid again. This is scary but so much fun all at the same time. Lola packs her bag with three notebooks full of writings and random short stories before brushing her teeth as she prepares for the writing group. Most of the stories are ones she'd written between group therapy sessions or even at Rosewood. She feels unexpectedly nervous as she double checks that she's packed her most interesting short stories and poems; the ones she wrote those first few days at Charlotte's house. She wishes Maria was here to talk to but reminds herself she has to learn to do things on her own. Clare could have helped her pick an outfit and Zoe would have known what to do about Aaron. *You have to learn to do this by yourself. Tim wants a merge. And he's serious this time.*

Aaron had offered to pick her up for the meeting, but she feels more comfortable meeting him there. The kiss has made things complicated. She's still waiting on a referral to another doctor and, until then, she doesn't want to risk getting him in trouble. He promised a writing group is okay. He said it will be therapeutic for her. She knows it'll be a lot more therapeutic than sitting alone at home, thinking about her mother's grave or whether or not to meet up with her birth father. She isn't sure how she'd handle a large social gathering of normies without Aaron by her side. For that, she's thankful. He's really been good to her, she decides.

Lola quickly forgets her worries as she settles in to her seat at a round table in the library. The group is as friendly as Aaron had promised. It consists of Denise, a 35-year-old single mother of three, Bob, a retired Marine she instantly likes because he had spent many nights in the military writing by flashlight and reminds her of Roy, Mason, a plumber with a passion for science fiction who is a lot like Rabbit, Piper, a middle-aged homemaker, and, of course, Aaron.

Lola listens with admiration as Denise reads her short story about a military man charged with murder. The detail she was able to put into the short piece gives it credibility. *How can she possibly know so much about military law? That must have taken a ton of research. Maybe research is what I need to be focusing on. ...What will they think of my work? Maybe they'll let me take a pass on sharing like they do in group therapy because it's only my first night.*

Bob isn't nearly as easily impressed. Lola gulps and tries not to make eye contact as he explains to Denise that it "just wouldn't happen that way." He tells her to make it

133

more realistic and bring her revised story back next week. *Geesh. How does she not cry? Maybe he's not so great. Maybe he's just mean. Or maybe it's PTSD.* Somehow, Denise takes Bob's criticism in stride, asking for details on what didn't make sense to him. His suggestions are kind and helpful and Lola is relieved to see that he isn't as gruff as he'd first come off. *Maybe I'll be able to read in front of the group after all,* Lola tells herself, even if it is a lie. *They'll have to go easy on me,* she reasons. *I'm new. They can't scare me off too fast. Clare could do this like a pro. Zoe, too. But I'm not alone, Aaron's here.*

An hour later, Lola isn't sure if they are just being nice or if they really enjoyed the work she shared. Her short story, *The Mills*, is about a teen runaway desperately searching for her father. A street kid, the protagonist possessed survival skills Lola only wishes she had; skills she wishes she could employ in her own everyday life. That's what she enjoys about writing. It isn't much different from going inside of yourself and creating a fake world and fake voices. With writing, it is acceptable to escape reality. People don't call you nuts for it.

"I love how you described her. I could see it. Her dreadlocks. The hem on her jeans," Piper says. "Thank you for sharing with us, Lola. It's so nice to hear a new voice in the group."

Lola wants to pinch herself to make sure she is real and not an alter when Piper uses that expression – "new voice." For the first time since leaving Rosewood, Lola feels like she belongs.

What impresses Lola most about the group is their range of talent. Their friendly banter is infectious and reminds her of family dinner nights at her mother's house. She is grateful Aaron invited her and tells him so as they walk out of the library together at the end of the night. Strolling past rows and rows of books, Lola is aware that their pace is sluggish at best. It's as if reaching the double glass doors of the library will signal a goodbye neither is ready for.

"I loved what you read of *Dreamers*," Lola says, sincerely.

"Oh yeah? That was new for me. I usually write things that are a lot darker. Something just inspired me, so I went for it. That's why they were laughing at me. I think they think I'm nuts," Aaron says.

Lola shivers at the word "nuts." It will never be possible for him to forget how they met, even when he does retire. She's not sure she can live with that long-term.

"I'll just be happy to get to a point to have a "normal" genre for me," Lola says. "The writing thing is so new to me. It's intimidating."

"Intimidating how?" Aaron asks, his thin eyebrows creasing.

Lola shrugs.

"Everyone was just so talented. And half of them have writing degrees," she says.

Aaron laughs.

"Correction: Everyone *thinks* they are so talented. As for the degrees? I have a theory about that. I think people with only writing degrees have nothing to write about. I think a better way is to get a degree in another field so that they have knowledge in another area to write about. I mean, how many books about writing are there? The market is flooded," he says. "Of course, this may just be how I justify my own, non-writing, degrees. I guess what I'm saying is that to be a good writer, you actually have to *live*. You can't just go off technical skills alone."

Lola laughs, seeing his point, but also his humility. She finds it endearing that he could be so talented and not have a swollen head pumped up with his own self-importance. She wonders what he thinks of her life. Has she lived or does it not count because she's spent most of it in a mental hospital?

"I see your point on that," she says, refocusing and thinking of her own draw to write about psychology. *Shit, you could write a memoir. You've got more knowledge about the loony bin than anyone,* she tells herself.

"Well, I'm so glad you came," Aaron says, exhaling as they get too close to the front doors to ignore them any longer. He stands with a straight back, like he isn't sure he is prepared to step into the cold night. But it isn't the chill he is afraid of, Lola doesn't think. The cold didn't stop him the night he kissed her on Charlotte's steps. Instead, she senses he doesn't want to leave their conversation any more than she does.

"It was really lovely, Aaron. Thank you for inviting me," she says.

"Membership is open, you know. You can come back next week. I think everyone really liked having you here," he says. "I could pick you up this time. Or, well, you could meet me here. No pressure or anything."

Lola feels her cheeks turn the color of Valentine's Day. An odd jab of pleasure—or maybe it is fear—knots in her abdomen. *What would Zoe do?*

"Yes. I'd like that," she says, playing with her hair. "It's a really cool group." *"Cool group." Really Lola? He's not a mental patient. You could have picked a more intelligent word. At least it sounded casual, I guess.* The color of her cheeks is already giving away too much, she is sure. *Stop over thinking. He's a person, not a monster. He cares about you. He's the guy who helped you all this time. You're okay. Play this cool. Remember, you are just getting to know him on a new level. Stay cool.*

Chapter Seventeen
Lola

Something strange is happening. It's like I'm watching myself in a movie. I have to write it down, as if it's a story, to make sense of it. I refer to myself as a third person. My new psychiatrist tells me this is normal, when you're going through a merge. It will take time, he says, for it all to work out. Meantime, this is a way to process it. So I'm going with it. I'm making my life into a book. Every night, when I get home, I just pull out my laptop and write it, as though it happened to some other woman named Lola. Someday, I hope I get closer to feeling it. This is unsettling. Here's what I've written in the past few days. If you care. If anyone does. I can't reach the alters…

Lola showed up at Aaron's promptly at 7 p.m. She was glad she'd left a little early. She'd had to drive slowly, with children still out–past dark–playing in driveways. She smiled at the whole-hearted feel of the place and remembered similar fall evenings in her childhood neighborhood playing light tag with friends. She and Aaron had planned to meet at his house and go to the movies together after ordering out. She was excited to see where he lived; imagining his home being covered floor to ceiling in books. At the same time, it was still awkward for her, trying to figure out his new role in her life. *He said we could take it as slow as I needed to.*

The quaint home was well lit and Rocky was the first to greet her, barking loudly and pushing against the door, anxious to get to the newcomer so that he can say hi. He was exactly as Aaron had described; big and "super friendly."

"Awww, you're okay, Big Dog," she said, hearing Aaron's footsteps not far behind.

"Rocky, be polite! Get down. Sorry, Lola, come on in," he said, opening the door and pushing the mutt out of the way.

His house smelt of mangos and peaches. Not a fan of fruit, Lola appreciated the sweet smell anyway. Lola had to take a second look at two pink jackets hanging in the mudroom of Aaron's home. At first glance, she got nervous; thinking these belonged to a wife or girlfriend. But she reminded herself of his daughters and relaxed quickly as he ushered her into the kitchen. *Why does it take so long to connect to these things? What's making me so suspicious? Stop being paranoid. You're supposed to act like yourself, not one of the alters.*

Aaron offered Lola a tea. Peppermint, Stella's favorite. He gave her a tour of his home while it cooled. While it was much different than she'd expected—with only a tiny bookcase in the corner of the living room—she was surprised at how homey it was. She wondered how much of the hominess was left over from Caroline and how much of it was all Aaron. She'd never known men to be capable of creating such warm spaces. But then, she'd never really known men in a domestic capacity at all. In fact, she remembered, Caroline had never lived here. The warmth was all Aaron.

She admired the photographs that hung in Aaron's den. Some were of his daughters – both beautiful girls who clearly loved their father based on the way they looked at him. Others were of his parents. Many were of Rocky. She liked that he liked animals – real and totem. She wondered if Rocky did for him what the alters did for her.

"It's a wonderful home, Aaron. So warm," she said.

"I try to keep it nice for the girls," he said. "If it was just me, it'd be a lot different," he said. "But they'd ride me if I lived like a bachelor."

Lola laughed.

So it was the girls who did it. Makes sense.

"I called for Thai. Is that okay? I still have time to change it if you'd rather go for pizza or Chinese," Aaron said.

"Thai is great," Lola said, suddenly missing Clare, whose favorite was Thai.

"Well sit down! Make yourself comfortable," he said. "The food won't be here for at least a half hour. I figured we have plenty of time before the movie."

The pair talked about everything they could imagine except the elephant in the room. Instead of talking about Lola's time at Rosewood or the kiss, they did as they had been; avoided it all. They talked about the writing group, their latest writing plans, Aaron's novel, Lola's plans to maybe write a memoir or non-fiction type work, the joy of writing poetry as therapy, and Rocky's latest run in with a random squirrel in the yard.

It was starting to feel a little ridiculous to avoid the obvious, but still. Lola wasn't sure what to make of this and wondered if she should bring it up. She had a feeling he felt the same.

How long will we tip toe around this? Is this healthy? Maybe he's just being respectful. That's not a bad thing at all.

"...or a romantic comedy. It's fine with me whatever you want to see. I just really wanted the excuse to spend time with you," Aaron said. "I've missed you."

Lola gulped.

He missed me? Maybe he really is okay with my being a loon. It's only been a couple of days.

"I missed you too. Let's do the romantic comedy," Lola said, because that was the only choice she'd heard.

"Ok, great, that gives us an hour and a half."

They ate their food in silence. It wasn't because there wasn't anything to talk about. It was because the food was delicious and the silence even more tasty. For their own reasons, it was nice to just sit and enjoy each other's company without constant chatter clouding the space between them.

The movie was perfect for a date. About an older couple looking for a second chance at love, Lola thought the similarities between the plot and she and Aaron were uncanny. She laughed and enjoyed his laugh at parts they'd already experienced together.

"That was great! I'm so glad we went to see it," Aaron said, taking her hand as he led her out of the theater to his car.

It was so fast and natural that it was like they'd been together for years. Lola's hand felt warm and safe in his and she wished he didn't have to let go when they finally made it back to his car.

Back at Aaron's house, the couple listened to country music while finishing off Thai leftovers. They sat on his couch, hand in hand, watching the news and debating politics. Having been out of the loop so long, Lola was fascinated by Aaron's impressions of the Republican Party since the Reagan Era.

But eventually, they ran out of other things to talk about. And just as Lola was getting anxious for Aaron to finally kiss her again, he brought up the dreaded subject.

"There's probably things we should talk about. First off, are you okay?" he asked. His voice was gentle but curious.

Fuck.

"Well, that's hard to explain," Lola said, watching his face for hints on how to respond.

When his eyes showed nothing but genuine interest, she dared to continue.

"It's scary," she said. "You have to understand that I don't have any experience with this sort of thing."

Aaron nodded. "I'm not a stranger. You can talk to me. And we don't have to do anything quickly. It's been nice, just keeping each other company. ...We don't have to talk about us. Why don't you tell me how things have been going at Rosewood in the PHP group?"

This is why I like him. Lola told Aaron all about Justin, Edna, Tina, and Lindsay's latest antics. She also told him about the random people from the substance abuse wings. Aaron listened without interrupting.

"So, does that mean you are okay now? I mean have you worked through everything?" he asked.

Lola sighed. She didn't know how to answer that one. She knew exactly what he was really trying to ask: Had the alters officially merged?

"Well, it means I've dealt with things. But I still have some work to do," she said. "I still have a therapist and that new psychiatrist you sent me to and I still go to group meetings. It's become sort of like a home base to me."

Aaron exhaled, looking relieved.

"That's really great. Really great. You're such a survivor, Lola. I can't imagine what your life has been like," he said. "I've known others who would not be able to put things back together the way you have."

"Oh? Who do you mean?" Lola asked, never one to take a compliment.

Now it was Aaron's turn to hesitate. He tried hard to get his words right in his head before he continued. He didn't want to say anything that would scare her off or offend her. He wished he hadn't brought the subject up.

"Caroline had a few issues of her own," he finally said. "I didn't know about them beforehand when we first met. But it is what got me into psychology. Everything happens for a reason, I guess. No regrets."

"Oh. I totally understand. Is she okay now?" Lola asked, not wanting to pry. She didn't have any real life experience in the area with ex-wives and made a mental note to discuss how this topic should be approached with Ann. Sometimes, she felt so behind her years.

Aaron's laughter interrupted her thoughts.

Why is that funny?

"With Caroline, 'okay' is a relative term. She's medicated and she's doing fine for now," he said. "But I don't hold my breath. She's bipolar. I never know when she's going to get manic and drop the girls on my doorstep and take off for God knows where. She isn't like you. No motivation to change."

"Has she done that before?"

"Taken off? ...I can't count how many times," he said.

"How does she have custody?" Lola asked.

Aaron laughed again.

"A few reasons I guess. A great lawyer, paid for by yours truly, for starters. She's a woman. I have daughters, not sons, and the court often likes to place kids with the same sex parent, the list goes on," he said. "I hate it but I do my best to stay as involved as I can in their lives. They know I'm here when they need me."

She was tempted to offer Aaron a hug but settled for a pat on his knee.

"I'm sorry," she said, staring at her hand, feeling like their roles had been flipped and not sure what to do about it. "The girls are really lucky to have you."

"Okay! Enough of this depressing stuff!" Aaron said. "Do you dance?"

Do I?

Lola smiled.

"I can try!"

"Great," he said, standing up and taking her hand.

* * *

"I haven't slept in three days. I'm starting to freak out that I'm going manic because it's not really bothering me," Huey said. "I feel like it *should* be bothering me but the project I'm working on is a lot of fun."

"What's the project?" Lola asked.

"I'm designing a website for a tee-shirt making company. They do screen printing and things like that. My brother-in-law owns it. He's letting me go at it however I want. I love when I get a project where I have free rein. I've only got about a week to get it done, so sleep hasn't felt that important."

"Have you mentioned this to Dr. Pezanowski?" Ann asked.

PHP had started late today because of a fire drill at Rosewood in the locked wing. The group would barely have time for check ins. But Lola didn't mind. She didn't have much to say and was starting to feel like she was ready to move on to a less intensive group meeting schedule. Lola eyed Huey as he continued to talk about his work.

She admired the excitement in his face as he explained pixels and how photographs were formatted specifically for web work. He wore a red and black flannel shirt, and his hair was home to three massive cowlicks. Lola found his ruffled look attractive and was fascinated by the animation in his voice as he spoke.

It's too bad he's nuts too. Two crazies together. That wouldn't work. We would have too many relationships going on at the same time. Sucks. He's adorable. And, besides, Aaron's better. Stop being man-crazy. You're like a teenager. Or Zoe. God, I miss her.

"...else like to check in?" Ann asked.

Worried she'd been caught daydreaming, Lola stepped right in to update the group on her plan to start writing more. Maybe even try to get published one day.

"What do you want to write about?" Justin asked.

Lola shrugged.

"I haven't quite gotten there yet. I figure my writing group will help me to figure that out," she said. "I'm trying a little bit of everything. Even some really dark stuff."

"You know, Lola. If you really get into this writing thing, I'm going to need a lot of content for my websites," Huey said.

"Remind me to give you my business card."

Lindsay sneered and rolled her eyes.

"Get a room, guys," she finally said.

Everyone ignored her.

"That would be great, Huey, thanks," Lola said, trying to silence the butterflies in her stomach.

He's crazy too. Don't be an idiot! You have enough on your plate with Aaron.

"Cool."

"Are we okay?" Edna asked.

"Yes, Edna. You are okay," Ann said. Her answer was so second nature that her voice was literally monotone. Edna went right back to la-la land.

What does that poor woman think about? She's schizophrenic too. But that's also different than DID. I wonder if she has her own life inside of there and can't be bothered with us. That would be something to write about – what goes on in the mind of an old crazy lady. ...Wait, that's me.

"I *wish* I had Huey's manic going on," Tom said. "I'm in a low that I can't seem to shake. Just getting up to come here is killing me. I haven't been to work in days. If I'm not here, I'm sleeping or at AA. It's getting harder and harder not to use, and my sponsor says it's only a matter of time if something doesn't change."

"Nice sponsor! Get a new one," Lindsay said, suddenly plugged in. Lola suspected Lindsay had a crush on Tom. He was the only one she didn't criticize.

"I've run through sponsors like people change their underwear," Tom said. "There's no one new left, and Dr. Pezanowski says I need to stick with this one for at least a year."

"Oh. That sucks. Dr. Pezanowski is a douche," Lindsay said. "He thinks he's in charge of everyone and everything. I'm over him."

Tom laughed.

"What does using do for you?" Ann asked.

Lola recognized the question instantly as one of motivational interviewing from her borrowed readings from Aaron's psychology collection. *This will be interesting. Wish I had my notebook. This would be good material for a book about an addict.*

"What do you mean?" Tom asked.

"For thirty years, you've turned to drugs or alcohol to deal with your depression and other issues," Ann said. "That means these drugs *do* something for you. What do they do for you?"

"They help me escape."

"And how has escaping worked out for you?"

Lola smiled. She could see that question coming from a mile away. Ann was practicing classic substance abuse therapy here and it was interesting to watch.

"It hasn't worked out for me," Tom said, looking at the floor.

"So what are you going to change?" Ann asked.

"I have no fucking idea what I'm going to change. You tell me. Isn't that *your* job?" Tom asked.

"Oh come on! She's just a shrink. Give her a break! Shrinks never do the work. They make us do everything. They don't get it that it's their job to fix us. They expect us to fix ourselves," Lindsay said.

Lola wanted to scream at Tom and Lindsay. *How could anyone put their recovery in someone else's hands? The only way to truly recover was to want it for yourself. Why can't they understand that?* Instead of speaking, Lola bit her bottom lip and waited for Ann to speak.

"I'm wondering what gave you the impression that you weren't responsible for your own mental wellness, Lindsay?" Ann asked, on cue.

And Tom. Him too. Why did she leave him out?

"Because it's what you are paid to do. Not me! I don't get a dime for being here. Instead, I get to waste my inheritance helping to subsidize this!" Lindsay argued.

"You are here voluntarily," Ann said. "You could leave at any time. What does being in a wellness center do for you, Lindsay?"

Lindsay's face turned pink.

"Why don't you ask Tina, Edna, or Justin that? They've been here longer than I have!"

"Because I'm asking you," Ann persisted.

"Tina's not even paying attention!" Justin said. "And I love it here. Mostly. When Tina's not being mean to me."

"Tina? Are you with us?" Ann asked, cursing herself for not noticing that the teenager was tuned out again.

Tina clutched her iPod. She refused to even take the ear buds out of her ears.

"Look, music soothes me. Music is the one place where I feel understood," she explained. "My shrink knows this and he is cool with it. I don't get why there has to be different rules here."

"Here, we are practicing social interactions," Ann said. "It's pretty difficult to do that when one member is tuned out."

Tina blew a bubble. It popped on her face. She chased her gum back with her tongue. Finally, after about five minutes of the group watching her and no one speaking, she removed the earbuds.

"Fine," she said. "This is exactly why I hate it here. Too many rules."

I wonder if that's what Rabbit hated too.

* * *

Writers group went nothing like either had anticipated that week. Anxious to hear what each other had written about, Lola and Aaron both had last-minute reservations about sharing with the larger group; or, more accurately each other. They confessed this, walking in together, but not as clearly as they probably should have, they later decided.

It'll be fine. It's just fiction. He knows I'm new at this, just exploring. It's just an excerpt. Nothing to get worried about. Besides, he said he had trouble writing this week, too. Relax. Just listen. He's not my doctor

anymore and promised not to diagnose me.
Lola finally closed her eyes, listening to every word as writers took turns reading from their latest work.

When it was Aaron's turn to read, Lola didn't want to miss anything. She hoped, by listening to Aaron read from his latest novel, *The Game*, she'd learn something. She refused to think about her turn, which would be coming soon. She needed to be present, in the moment; something that would have been unimaginable only six months ago.

Aaron cleared his throat and paused, as if trying to memorize what he'd written, but finally content to just read from his lined notebook pages. His voice was slow and steady as he read:

"Excerpt from *The Game*. By Aaron Ross. ...I hope there's no God. 'Cause if there's God, it's forever winter. He knows 'bout my two lives: My two wives. The time I stomped a kitten's head into concrete 'cause I couldn't decide. He's counted notches on my bed. Me? I lost track in '73.

Memories come alive: The Vietnamese whores I paid to save: Helped survive. Just that kind of guy. The crumbly girl I wrapped round my leather belt to feel alive. I can still

155

smell her – apple pie and peppermint: A girl scout. Mine. She wore knee socks in July.

The IV leaks into my hand.

I remember rainstorms and the fried dough taste of summer. Fireworks. The pier. Playing chicken on the lake: Double dare. I wonder, is there heaven for them other kind? They go to church on Sundays, not just when mother or the grand kids stop by. They never swear or lie. Eating shortcake, roast beef, sweet peas.

"Sir? We need to call you wife."

Wives. I turn away, telling myself God is only make-believe. A fairy tale for the weak. "Don't need a wife to die."

"But Sir..." She cries.

I stare past her, through the blinds. Icicles grip the windows' edge, tight like gifts for grand kids on my dime. I look away. It's wintertime. A snowball fight. Can't be more than nine. He throws me in a snowbank. Ice bites my cheek. Blood trickles from my nose. I can't taste it. I stand, rubbing the gritty cold from my eyes, and chase him. "That's right! ...Run! You're mine."

The door opens. People walk in. Go away.

"Papa? It's me. Can you hear me?"

Kid, leave me alone, I'm tryin' here to die!

"Jimmy," my name falls off his lips, squeezing his hand tight.

"Papa, please don't die!"

Papa and his leather skin: The time he taught me how to fish, proud of my four-inch pike. And "Boy, bait your own hook!" The time he taught me how to fight: "Keep um thumbs tucked in. Break um and they no good."

"Papa, don't go! I need you to teach me how to drive!" I beg of him.

He sighs, opening his eyes.

He looks at me, terrified, then through me. I cannot understand why.

"Papa?"

He stares past me out the window. Snowflakes flutter by, reminding me of the time we built a snow fort so big it didn't melt til May and "that's my boy!"

I hope there's a God. If there's God, it's forever fishin' time. Where Papa can fish and brag to the other guys, adding extra inches: "Room to grow, Boy." I'm five feet, five. I hope Papa's right. And I wonder, what will I do when it comes time to ask a girl out? How will I survive, without...

"Papa!"

"What, Boy?" God dammed kid.

He's with me now. I think, if he could, he'd hit me. (Thumbs in just right).

'Please don't die.'"

Lola didn't know what to think. She wanted to grab the notebook from Aaron's hands before he even had a chance to close it. As he looked up for group feedback, they caught eyes. Lola looked down, a glow spreading across her face but no idea why. *What does that mean? He doesn't believe in God? He's been a bad person? He's lost someone? What does it all mean? I need context. Is this fact or fiction? And, why, do I need so badly to know? Oh my God. What will he think of mine? Mine's even worse. What was I thinking? I sound more morbid than Rabbit in mine...*

Lost in thought, Lola barely heard what the group said about Aaron's work. *There's no way that I can explain that Rabbit's merged into me and she's the one writing this horror. They aren't going to recognize this side of me. It's not how everyone sees me.* Aaron gently nudged her arm, signaling her turn to read—clockwise—from her own work in the circle. Panic gripped her chest and it took everything in her not to run out of the room. Like a robot on autopilot, probably from all the practicing she'd done with Charlotte, she started reading her own work; nearly memorized. She didn't look up once, breathless, from start to finish reading:

"Pretty Little Feet, a short story and first attempt only, by Lola Murray. ...**Hoodoo legend will tell you that it's not just the left hind foot of a rabbit that's lucky. The foot's gotta come from a rabbit shot or otherwise captured in a cemetery. It's true. I'm a lot of things, but not a liar. You can look it up on Wikipedia if you don't believe me. And if you have that kind of time. There are other superstitions too. Some say that you have to do it in a full moon, or a new moon. Others say it matters whether or not the rabbit is alive. They say it has to be on the 13th or a rainy day. At least a Friday.**

Not me. I don't believe any of that. You see, I've been doing this a long time. I've studied all the ways. I've got my own ideas about what makes a rabbit's foot lucky. But we'll get to that. We have all kinds of time. It takes at least five minutes for them to really bleed out. Except that last one, she was a fighter. Just my type. Or not. I change my mind on that from year to year.

* * *

I admit it. I like it rough. A simple fetish isn't about to scare me. I've been that way since I was sixteen and my high school boyfriend spanked me on his parent's waterbed between English and Chemistry. What I would give to go back to those days; his warm hands, eager eyes. Two kids, a dozen rubbers, good porn, a flogger and a pack of Lucky Strikes. Everything flashes in front of me. I don't have a lot of time, so I'll get to the point. I've never been afraid of my sexuality. I figure, use it while you can. Use it good.

I probably should have known better. My friends warned me. My father, too. But why listen to a man who only showed up when I turned eighteen and it was too late for Mom to go after him for child support? Not much of a daddy there. More like sperm donor. I wonder if things would have been different, had he been around. Who could really blame me for answering the advertisement? Not like "Daddy" was going to pay tuition. I mean, what girl in her right mind turns down a free mani-pedi from a harmless old guy? I guess I'm just unlucky. "Sugar Daddy, please apply" and "Seeking Arrangement." Only, there was no sugar to this daddy.

Me: I take what I can get. You see, I've been doing this a long time. I've met hundreds of guys. Fuck you, "Daddy." You too, Mom, with your parade of men. It'll be different for me, I told myself. And it has been. I've always taken precautions. Googled them, told friends where I'd be, met in public places, used safe words, even made them take pictures of their licenses. But Mr. "Jack Rabbitt"--how did I ever believe that was really his name?—said he was a widow. I didn't see any harm in meeting him at the cemetery. He told me he wanted to show me his wife's grave; said it was their anniversary. I felt bad for him. I mean, the guy was ancient. Like fifty.

* * *

I started collecting in 1993. I've gone through all the colors of the rainbow, and back, twice. I'm back to indigo; the perfect combination of azul, purple, and fuchsia. I need to get back to the craft store for more Rit Dye. Ain't nothing like a rainbow to make a man feel—finally—lucky. Too bad I can't take the feet out with me, to the store. At least I can't lose them, all lined up on my shelf. They say losing um is bad luck. Not for me. Not no more. Jack Rabbitt is not a loser. Fuck you, "Dad." What do you think of me now, Old Man? You watchin this shit?

How do rabbits compare to women? Well, don't get me started. My late wife—whore that she was—is the perfect example of this. For one, they breed. You try getting excited about a namesake and having it come out three shades of pigment too dark to ever be called your own without snickers from the guys at the station. Fuck that.

Rabbits, like women, are tricksters. Ain't nothing like a pretty woman to ruin a man's dreams, take his land, and leave him nothing but memories. A man, a smart one anyway, has got to make memories of his own. So every year, on the anniversary of the day the broad finally left me, I go hunting. Tonight was no different. Pretty little thing. Pretty little feet.

* * *

The mani-pedi wasn't even that great. Mr. Rabbit had made a special request; that he call and pick out the polish ahead of time. I don't like purple, no matter how fancy of a word you want to use for it. I should have argued, or just never shown up for the appointment. I'm more of a French manicure type of girl. But I wasn't about to put up a fight. Indigo was his wife's favorite color, the color of the dresses at their wedding, he said. Like I said, I felt sorry for the guy.

It doesn't matter what color, I suppose. Now, everything's red. Like that old boyfriend's sheets, the first time he took me home. I remember how he bawled them up and shrugged; told me not to worry about it. Promised he'd wash them himself, so his mother and sister wouldn't see. Asked to go again. "Just one more time." That one time became three, and back again.

Men, and boys, are all the same when you think about it. They only want one thing. It's what I've counted on. It's how I've paid my way through community college looking good and eating free. I haven't paid for a meal in over a year. Now, I wish I'd done things differently; seeing as there will be no more. I'm beginning to drift, and feel no pain. Red swirls at my feet. I wonder if he'll clean it up; hide it from authorities.

* * *

Stupid bitch. All she had to do was listen to me. I might have let her go. I actually kind of liked her. Called herself "Daddysgirl1985." I've done that before—set um free—when I ran out of dye. But not this time, she's too much of a fighter. Argued all the way home. I told her I just wanted to be able to see them in the light—the fancy toes I paid for. "No, not tonight," as if she had a choice. And then, she gave up the fight. I'm not sure I liked her as much then. It doesn't matter.

Chained to a wall in my basement. Like the others before. Squirming and trying to reason with me. "Sorry, bitch, but your tits aren't that great, and I'm not in it for those anyway. Breeder." What is it with women who think that a quick tongue and willingness to swallow will get them somewhere further? If I wanted that, I could pick it up for twenty roses and a whole lot less risk and hassle. Dye ain't cheap. Neither is gasoline.

Stupid me. I'm out of fuchsia, too. Getting sloppy. I guess it happens to the best of us, with time. I watch her, motionless, except her chest, still moving up and down. Heaving, if she had more fight. More like conceding. Pathetic. It won't be long now. I can see her surrendering. I feel myself grow hard. I adjust. I don't want to admit to myself that there's something kinky about that moment when fate surrenders and destiny falls to its knees. I refuse to call this a fetish. I touch myself anyway. A man has needs.

* * *

Silly, silly me. I should have told Kate where I was going. They'll never find me or the dozens who've come before. I need this to go fast. He's staring at me. Sick, sick man. I tell myself not to fight it. There's no point in arguing. I know this by the jars—tiny painted toes, missing the big one so there's four—and colors that surround them. I wonder what he does with them, the big ones. It doesn't matter.

At least I can't feel it anymore. My eyes are closed, head is back, and I'm ready to move on. I don't want to see what becomes of the rest of me. If he could do that to my foot – my feet? I can't leave. I want to take all that's left of me and scream. I want to ask him why and make him, too, bleed.

He sits there in a chair, sipping coffee, chewing nicotine. I want to spit. On him. At him. I want to hop up on my right foot and hit his growing bulge. He sits there, getting off to my silent prayer for it to be over. I lay there, on a cold floor, chained to a wall, wondering if it ever will be. Reminding myself that I did this to myself. I've always been good at owning my own shit and admitting when I was wrong. I should have trusted my gut when he asked me to come home with him "just to show off those pretty little feet." I thought there might be something in it for me. I mean, nothing wrong with a few roses. I told myself, he just wanted company. I would have given him more than that. Chains don't scare me.

* * *

Getting um here isn't as easy as you might think. There are ways you have to do it, so you don't get caught. Two decades and no one has a clue. They just go missing. Pretty little girls with perfect tidy lives, never to be seen again; unlucky little things. I'm not a gambling man, as funny as that may seem. I don't take chances. And, well, I have luck on my side. Times twenty-two, now twenty-three. I only keep the left ones. The right ones? I eat. Like rabbit meat.

She chokes on saliva. I chuckle, remembering how that whore spit in my face and told me I'd make a horrible father anyway. I'm tempted to cover her mouth with my hand, just to watch her eyes bulge. But that would take the fun out of it; watching the struggle. I look at my watch. Two more minutes. If I'm lucky, three. I already miss her screams. Her black eyes, wide, and staring at me as I fondled her feet. A good pair of ankle restraints and there ain't nothing to it. Who has time for rope? Please. Not me. Not anymore.

I close my eyes and stroke it off, thinking about the last time that whore fucked me. She rode me into another planet. I had no idea it wasn't my seed. Took her three minutes. Maybe less. No woman could ever get me off like that. Not without pantyhose and feet. Jack Rabbitt style, she took me. Lucky me. Shoulda made her bleed.

* * *

Dying isn't as hard as you might think. Looking back, I can't say I have a lot left to live for anyway. Cranked out mom and a half-brother twice as bad. The high school guy traded me in years ago for a girl who had a better ass. Funny, he used to say she was ugly when I was feeling insecure. But all men—and boys—are the same. Like rabbits, hoping from one bed to another; breaking hearts. They don't care about the bruises they leave on us, the stains on their sheets, or anything more than getting lucky.

He chokes his cock like he's on the clock. If I could, I'd yawn. I don't have time for this. There are places to see and things to do. He didn't give me time or room for goodbyes. I'm not sure who will even care, when I die. So it's okay. I wonder what it will be like, in heaven or in hell; wherever I'm headed. I refuse to live with regrets. I'm not that kind of girl.

I exhale one final time, feeling myself lift fully from the floor. No man has ever lifted me higher, not without suspension rods and the threat of a crop. I look down at him, lonely old man, and smile. Color blinds my eyes. It comes in every color: red, orange, yellow, green, blue, purple, indigo. Indigo. Indigo."

* * *

When breathless Lola finally looked up from her notebook, she couldn't help but notice Denise's open mouth.

"Wow."

Lola said nothing, unsure of what that may mean. She didn't hear most of the comments from other writers, who all encouraged her to consider horror as her genre of choice. Instead, she mostly stared at the floor, unable to look at Aaron, until it was time to leave. She felt naked, something she'd secretly hoped to be with him for a while now, but not this way. *Idiot. It was too much. They know you are crazy now.*

"You ready, killer?" Aaron said an hour later, smiling, after most of the group had already packed their things for the night and was digging in for last minute hits on cold coffee and stale donuts.

"Yes."

"Okay, let's get out of here."

"Your place or mine? Charlotte and crew aren't home tonight."

"Let's go to mine. I'm a little worried about what kind of snacks you have in the freezer," Aaron teased. "Or, worse, bedroom."

"Funny. I was kind of worried about that. You thinking something."

"Naw, don't be. It was fun. It's all good. Just fiction. We can talk about it later."

"Okay. Let's do that. Tonight was ... intense,"

"Indeed. But, Lola, intense never scared me."

Lola laughed, loud. "Clearly."

Chapter Eighteen
We

Lola

It's been nearly a year since our full merge. Progress is slow and not without its scary moments, like the stories Aaron and I write together now. But it's steady. I'm still getting used to saying 'I' instead of 'we.' So, for now, I'm sticking with we. At least I can talk about myself in the first person again. With the writing, it will take more time. But it's a heck of a start; less complicated.

The thing is, the alters will always be a part of me. In a way, it will always be we. I'm glad about that. Each of them is a big part of who I am today. They'll always be with me. I'm living for all of us and I'll never forget that. They gave up their lives for me.

Some days are better than others. I get lonely, sure. But I have friends and family for those days. I try to remind myself that they aren't really gone, there just more a part of me now – like they should have been in the first place.

Zoe would be pleased to know that Aaron has retired to focus on his writing and research and we are slowly building something special. I don't know where it will lead, but I did get to meet Sage this week. She's a lovely girl and Maria would like her. I'm looking forward to meeting Abby, too. I'm not rushing anything. I have all the time in the world now.

We attend a regular writing group together and spend our free time doing crossword puzzles--the kind Zoe used to steal for Frog.

When I get sad about the alters, Aaron reminds me that they are like totem animals now--always with me and always sending little reminders of what's important to us; to we. I'll never forget the first time he tried to talk to me about totem animals. I wanted to strangle him. But now, I see the value in it. It's a metaphor for how all living things share commonalities in this great big, complicated world.

I still attend a partial hospitalization program. I probably could get out of it. But I think it's important. I never want to forget the people I met at Rosewood, who, like me, were just stuck and trying to figure things out. I'll keep going as long as my insurance covers it.

I have my own place now. It's small and nothing to really brag about. But it's all mine. I have one wall for each alter – a place where I keep mementos and things that remind me of them so I never forget. In my bedroom is a wedding frame for Zoe and Roy with hearts on it. Maybe, someday I'll fill it. In my tiny kitchen hangs a mission statement Tim made us complete just before the final merge. I read it in my writing group and people looked at me like I was crazy. For the first time, I didn't care. We're all a little crazy. I read it every day as a reminder:

We
by us (me)

We are united as it was always meant to be
We are the child that was Sam –
protected and loved by mother Maria and father Tim.
We are the sadness that was Rabbit –
alone and afraid but not fearful to admit it.
We are the strength that was Clare –
a best friend to ourselves in times of trouble.
We are the love that was Zoe and Roy –
sometimes, quiet and sometimes loud.
We are the thinker that was Frog –

hopeful dragonflies.
We are Lola Lee Murray.
Together, we are strong.

I never got to say goodbye to Rabbit, Clare and Frog. I think it would have been too hard. With Clare, anyway. But they're always with me. I'll never shed a tear without knowing Rabbit is with me. I can't laugh without hearing Clare. And thinking, well, that's all I ever do. There's no way to forget Frog.

It makes me happy, knowing Sam got the normal family she always wanted before it was time to go. I like to think of her in Disneyland. I know she's spending her free time chasing Peter Pan and Simba. Just last week, I made Aaron take me to the new Nemo movie, just in case she was in there somewhere, watching. He said he was excited. And I could tell he was. He seems to have a thing for fish. But then, it's Aaron. He has a thing for all animals.

Every time he kisses me, I know Zoe would be squealing in delight. I hope Roy kisses her every night, before bed, need it or not. To me, that's true love. Maria and Tim? I don't worry about them. I never did. It wasn't my job. I'm glad they no longer have to worry about me and can focus on each other and Sam. I can't say I don't look for

Maria every time I want advice. Now, I go to Mom's grave—even alone—to talk to her. The dragonfly makes me smile. Even in death, she's calling me that silly name, and I love it: My very own totem.

It's funny. All those years locked up. Every med you can imagine. All those doctors, hypnosis, EMDR, meditation, yoga, diet changes and therapists. More talking and talk therapy than any one person could ever be expected to do in a lifetime. All of it. Yet none of it worked. All of that and the answer was in front of us all along: Fill the holes, and boom, a merge.

Of course, it took fifty-two years to figure that out. I expected some big explosion. I expected fireworks. But it was simple. They just drifted off, hand in hand, together. I couldn't even watch it. It just seemed too sad, but also too unreal. It was like watching someone fall asleep or fade into a peaceful sunset. Aaron says they are like fish that found their water. He says a little birdie told him that, but I suspect I know who that was.

I think about my father. I wonder if his fish are swimming in a pond. I've let go of my anger and wish him well. If anyone gets how complicated this stuff is, it's me.

I'll never be off medication. I wouldn't trust it. I still go to PHP once a week, need it or not. I think of it as getting myself a tune up. I do it like I do my writers' group. The fact is, the people at Rosewood are as much family to me as the alters are; always will be. So, I'm getting there. One day at a time. And, I'm happy. I hope the others are, too. But they must be. How can I be sure? Because they *are* me now.

It's so simple when you get your head around it, pun intended. Every person in the world has many facets to their personality. We all have that evil side that comes out in traffic on the interstate or after waiting far too long in a line. We also have that compassionate side that pulls over for a person stranded on the side of the road or puts money in the Salvation Army collection bin at Christmas. Our funny sides come out when we're in a good mood or just want to burn steam. And everybody cries. Everybody has those days where they feel like giving up. It was the same with me and the alters. Only, I named them.

Okay, I admit, it's a little strange that I heard them as actual voices. Ya'll can shoot me for that. But I do have a schizophrenia diagnosis too, so it's not so odd when you think of that. And that disease is hereditary; which is more likely to explain my father and probably what he actually had. I'll never know for sure. There's no reason to. I hear he's happy, too.

It's half past three. I need to get moving. I have group and today we're doing an awesome exercise. Be nice to yourself, and all of your personalities. You don't have to name them, and I don't advise you to. Just treat them with kindness and be your own best friend. I promise, they will thank you if you listen close enough.

***

The Rosewood PHP group therapy room is buzzing as people make their way in with music lyrics and audio devices in hand. Tina is skipping, something Lola has never seen before and doubts she'll ever see again. She has to give Ann credit for the assignment to find a song that represents the person picking it. Banter begins around who picked what song as the group waits for the therapist to filter in nearly twenty minutes late.

They agree to skip a traditional check-in and go straight to homework. The rules of the exercise are simple: To share all the songs without commenting on them in between and to later go back and process why those songs were chosen. The elimination of crosstalk will make for everyone to have the chance to get their song in.

Justin is enthusiastic to share his homework assignment first. He'd spent all night with Tina working on picking out just the right song to describe himself and finally settled on Justin Timberlane's "Bringing Sexy Back."

"Pleasssssse can I go first?" he begs, bouncing in his chair. "My song is the best!"

"Dude, no one cares. Go first," Tom says, rolling his eyes.

"No, guys, you're gonna like this," Tina says, more engaged in group than ever.

Lindsay leans forward in her chair. "Well get on with it," she says.

It reminds Lola of the way the alters used to fight and, for a moment, she misses them. She reminds herself that they will never be gone. They are part of her now. They always have been. She repeats this to herself like Tim's mission statement mantra.

"I picked 'Bringing Sexy Back!' But that's only 'cause Tina didn't have "I'm Too Sexy,'" Justin says.

"Well, *someone's* perked up," Lindsay says. "Last week you were all whiney and saying you'd never get a girlfriend. Someone's changed his tune. The magic of Rosewood, people."

As the group laughs, Justin begins singing his song. At first, Lola is afraid he'd have another freak out. It happens a lot with Justin. But instead, he leaps into the middle of the therapy circle and continues his performance, gyrating his hips.

"I'm bringing sexy back. Them other boys don't know how to act. I think you're special, what's behind your back? So turn around and I'll pick up the slack," he belts.

When he's done, he smiles at Lola, takes a bow, and sits back in his seat, handing the invisible talking stick to Tom. The group can't help but cheer and hoot for the innocent, fun-loving boy they've all come to love.

Tom, who chose "Manic Depression" by Jimmi Hendrix, goes next and the mood changes nearly as fast as his own often does. Tom is a rapid cycler.

Lindsay picks "Cry Baby" by Janis Joplin but then asks to change hers to "Material Girl" by Madonna after playing it for the group on her IPad.

For Tina, it's Papa Roach's "Last Resort."

She reads the words slowly, as if for dramatic impact, "…cut my life into pieces. This is my last resort, suffocation, no breathing. Don't give a fuck if I cut my arms bleeding. Do you even care if I die bleeding? Would it be wrong; would it be right? If I took my life tonight, chances are that I might…"

Huey, who admits he hasn't given any thought to the assignment because he was up all night working on a new site, is able to come up with a song on the spot. He picks "Unwell" by Matchbox 20 and recounts his favorite lines for the group.

"It goes 'I'm not crazy, I'm just a little impaired. I know, right now you don't care. But soon enough you're gonna think of me. And how I used to be, me…" he says.

Lola laughs. She can totally relate. Sharing at least one diagnosis has always made her feel a certain kindship with Huey. She smiles at him and mouths "good pick."

When it's finally her turn, Lola pulls out her song. She'd chosen Natasha Bedingfield's "Unwritten." The choice was obvious the second Ann gave out the assignment. And, for once, Lola had been able to make a decision on her own; not by committee or vote.

With everyone finished sharing their songs, Ann encourages people to talk about why they'd made their choices they had. For most, it's obvious. The group members know each other pretty well from meeting three times a week for several hours at a time. But some are less obvious. And some bring to light concerns.

"My worry is that you are still feeling suicidal, Tina," Lola says.

Tina rolls her eyes.

"Of course that's your worry. That's always your worry. Maybe if you stopped worrying about other people and focused on yourself you wouldn't be so fucking nuts!" Lola 's former hospital roommate says. "You sound like that Maria person in your head. You aren't my mother."

Lindsay laughs.

Lola considers Tina's words. She knows the young girl is right. She makes a mental note to try not to worry about Tina and to leave that to Ann. Part of her new beginning will be about letting others do their own work, she decides. She wishes she could check with Maria to be sure she has it right. She reminds herself of the mission statement mantra: *We are Lola Murray. Together, we are strong. Together, we are full.*

"You know what, Tina?" Lola asks. "You're exactly right."

Tina snaps her gum and smirks at Lola.

"Then tell us the point of your song, 'cause I don't get it," Tina says.

"Well, I guess what I was trying to say with my song is that I feel like I have a blank page. I have two choices. I can let my hospitalization and diagnoses define me or I can do something else. I've finally decided what I'm going to do and now I'm looking forward to doing it," Lola announces, triumphantly. "Basically, I'm in charge of my own destiny – no one else."

"That's great, Lola. Good for you," Huey says, sincerely.

"But how *would* you define yourself?" Lindsay asks. "I mean how can you suddenly take all that away and just say you aren't crazy?"

Lola smiles.

"I can't take away my past. I wouldn't want to. I loved my alters and I know they loved me. I'm going to use my past—and them—to help me. I'm not planning on writing my new chapters in permanent marker," she says. "I know I need room to grow. I'm going to let myself do that, however it looks. What's meant to be will be. Besides, I have you guys to help me."

***

The ride home from group is a peaceful one. Instead of hearing voices, Lola brainstorms ideas about the novel she's determined to write. Spending time with Aaron has helped her develop her passion for writing and she enjoys dreaming up plot lines almost as much as he. Today, she has a new idea.

She decides to blow off the grocery store, for now, on the way to her new apartment. She can always snack on cereal before running out to prep for dinner for herself and Aaron, later. She wants to get started on her new life.

She sits on her couch, not unlike the one she sat on so many times in so many therapists' offices all those years and flips open her laptop. She props herself up on a pillow, embroidered with dragonflies. Alone, at last, she writes:

Love Like Crazy: How I Got a Life at 53

It felt nice to have her own place and be able to entertain without Charlotte hovering. She'd worked hard over the past few months to make it her own. She'd finally unpacked all the boxes from the back rooms and had even managed to paint. She'd chosen neutrals; not ready to commit to anything bolder just yet. She figured she had plenty of time. And she liked the calm it brought into the space.

She hoped Aaron would feel welcome. She laid out special fabric place mats and put sterling candle holders with indigo votive candles on the table. The fireplace glowed against the dimly lit room; its light dancing gently on the walls. As she looked around for last minute ways to spruce things up, she thought of her mother's cluttered house. Oh, how she missed her creativity every day and wondered if it would ever get easier to be without her.

Lola checked the chicken, pulled out the cookies and threw linguini in the boiling pot, just as Aaron texted to say he'd be there in ten minutes and ask if she needed anything. She smiled. He was perfect in every way. She hoped he felt the same about her but somehow doubted it.

If he was that into you, he'd have made a move. He sees you as a friend. Or maybe not. Tonight will tell.

She ran to the bathroom to brush her teeth and wash her face just in time for the doorbell to ring.

Aaron held a bouquet of red long stemmed roses. He presented them to her before she even had the door open, almost shoving them at her.

She laughed.

He seems nervous. This is good.

"Thank you! Come in!" Lola said, ignoring the awkwardness of the moment and gesturing toward the living room.

Aaron instantly walked to the fireplace.

"Oh, I love this!" he said, putting his hands up to the heat.

Lola put the flowers on her counter and joined him in front of the fireplace.

"I know. It's great. It's been so cold out lately." she said. "This warms the whole place up great. I barely have to pay for other heat."

Lola took Aaron's coat and sat him at the kitchen table, offering him warm cookies while she finished preparing their dinner. He consumed them like a kindergartner just home from school. It felt good to feed him. For so long, he'd been the one to take care of her.

After dinner, the couple sat down on the couch. Lola leaned against Aaron and was startled when she felt his body stiffen. Telling herself she'd just imagined it, she leaned in even closer as Aaron began to ramble.

"Denise said she is excited to see what your new ending will be on that short story," he said. "She called me today. Did you know that she once wrote a short story about a guy who kept wild animals in his yard as pets? Can you imagine the research that took? She's not even an animal person. Seems so odd to me."

"Wow. Weird." Lola said. "She hates cats; I know that much for sure."

"I don't like doing research, myself. I like writing about things I know. Maybe that's why I'm not into the science fiction stuff that much lately. I've been having a heck of a time with it."

"Yeah. I don't get that stuff either. Maybe it's because I spent so much time stuck in my head that I like to write about things that are more external or something. But then, how much do I really know about the outside world? I'm just starting to get the hang of it now. It's pathetic."

Shut up already! You never talk this much! Why is he so nervous? This is torture.

Lola casually slid her skirt up a little higher, hoping the sight of her naked thigh in the light of the fire would help him stop with the nervous chatter and get down to business. She watched for any sign that he'd noticed: *No dice. He'll never get over it. It was silly to think he would. He just sees me as an experiment. A nut. A crazy with a happy ending. Thank God Zoe isn't around so see this, she'd be a wreck.*

"I've been doing a lot of fun writing, though. I've been able to get back to my novel but I'm not sure I'm ready to share it with the group just yet. Sort of in the early draft stages."

Aaron began telling her about his latest chapter of "The Game." In it, the protagonist is faced with a horrible decision, he explained.

"Like a no-win decision. He just can't win either way. He's ..."

Lola found herself drifting. She could no longer pretend to focus on his words. She wanted to scream at the top of her lungs "What's wrong with me? Why won't you kiss me? Are kisses reserved for just one on my sister's porch?"

Maybe he just doesn't see me that way.

"That's great," she said, noticing he'd stopped talking and hoping it was the right thing to say.

"Lola? What's bothering you?" Aaron's eyebrows were thin and furrowed. He slid back from her, but his eyes never left hers. "Are you having, um, issues again?"

Great. Do I tell him? Do I make something up? No. You said you were going to be authentic. You said you were going to be honest. You've been brave so far. He hasn't let you down. Be fair and tell him. He has a right to know.

Lola's face grew hot. She could feel the color of Christmas rising in her neck, past her cheeks, all the way to her forehead.

"Um. Okay. Are you sure you want to know?"

Stop stalling. Tell him.

"Jesus, is it that bad? Are the alters back? You can tell me these things. You know I'll help you," Aaron said, unable to hide the alarm in his voice. "Or is it me? Did I do something wrong?"

"Oh! No! Not at all. You did nothing wrong. Not at all. It's not bad really. And the alters are gone. They really merged this time. Stop worrying about that. ...I guess I'm just confused. I mean, we spend all this time together. We've been out quite a few times and we talk every night. I'm always coming by when I can to say hi during the day. We have the writing group. We seem like we get along. Everything is good," she said.

"Okay. Now I'm the one who is confused. Isn't all of that good?" Aaron asked. "Is it too much for you? Do you feel smothered? Do you want me to give you some space? I know you're trying to establish your independence. I'd never want to intrude on that. I want that for you too!"

Lola laughed. The concern in his eyes was priceless.

This poor, poor man. My God. No wonder Caroline ate him alive. I need to go easy on him.

"No! It's not too much at all," she said. "I think that's the problem."

Aaron looked at her inquisitively.

"I don't understand," he said.

How the hell am I going to make this any clearer? Do I just kiss him myself? I don't even know how. What if it scares him? What if he doesn't feel the same? ...Shut up. You know he feels the same. He's just freaked out by the whole shrink thing. And the eight other people who might have something to say about it...

"Okay. I'm just going to be really blunt about this because I don't want to make you nervous. But I also don't want you to feel pressured, so here goes," Lola said. "I'm wondering why you've never tried to kiss me again."

Okay. You said it. Shut up. Wait. Let him speak. Don't fill the silence with babble. Play like Roy and wait quietly.

"Oh, Lola! I'm so sorry," Aaron said. "Do you think that means I'm not attracted to you? You're beautiful! I don't understand how you could not see it."

Lola shrugged.

"I'm honestly not sure what to think," she said, reminding herself of the dozens of times she'd caught him staring at her.

"Wow. Okay. I'm so sorry. Um. Well. I guess it's my turn to be blunt," he said. "This is harder than it seems. Okay. Well, remember when you told me about the merge?"

I fucking knew it. He's afraid that I'm too crazy.

"Yes."

"Well, I made a promise to Frog – before he left, I mean," Aaron's words stopped. For a split second, she thought she saw a flash of sadness on his usually passive, gentle face.

"Now I don't understand. What happened with Frog? What kind of promise?"

"Lola. I'm afraid to hurt you! I promised Frog I'd take care of you always. I don't want to take advantage of you or hurt you in any way. I never have, regardless of any promise to Frog or ethical obligation. I mean, I should never have kissed you in the first place. So I'm trying to behave. I want to help you make this transition and just, well, be there for you. It doesn't' mean I'm not tempted..."

It all made sense. The hesitations every time they went to say goodbye. The way Aaron would hold back or end their embraces. The way he'd put the roses between them just tonight, as if to avoid what would naturally and normally be a hello kiss.

Screw it.

Lola embraced her inner Clare, leaned over and planted her lips on his before Aaron had a chance to know what was coming. She was forceful about it, making him know that if anyone should be scared, it should be him. And he wasn't. He returned her kisses with a fury that could only have been built up in months of flirtations and unanswered attraction.

They made out on Aaron's couch for more than an hour, until Lola's face was raw from his scruffy beard. Finally, when they came up for air, Lola spoke first.

"Listen to me. And listen good. I am not afraid of you. I could never be afraid of you. You have helped me," she said. "I wasted 30 years on being crazy and listening to what other people thought or told me to do. No more."

Aaron pulled her closer.

"Yes, Ma'am. I second that. No more," he said, kissing her again even harder than before.

Lola felt, for the first time in her real--not internal--life, safe in a man's arms. Finally, she had the prescription that she needed: Live, Laugh, Love, daily, as needed. Repeat. The rest? Well, that could be figured out as she went. *After all,* she decided, *everyone's a little crazy.*

Acknowledgements

Thank you to my loyal readers, who took the time out of their lives to share in Lola's story and see it through until the end. The messages I've received from readers, some who suffer from DID, have been both uplifting and inspirational. Together, we can learn from one another and help reduce stigma around mental illnesses of all kinds. Like the alters in *Merge*, if we use our shared voices to educate and promote awareness, we have a shot at making the world a more colorful, empathetic, and safe place for all who suffer.

A shout out to Sharon Luxton, a reader from across the big pond, who reached out to me through social media and gave me the lift I needed to finish the series. Her love for Lola and crew kept me going. Thank you, Sharon! I promise to keep you reading about life's crazy journeys, one story at a time.

Special thanks to my author friends who serve as voices of reason and encouragement at just the right times. I could not continue to write about such tough topics without you. Your advice— even when you think I'm not listening— is something that I carry with me through each chapter, like Lola will always cherish her alters. Without you, I wouldn't have the courage to publish another word. It was you and your support who helped bring *Alters* to number one on amazon in its category. It's when the indie world merges that, together, we make magic.

As always, special thanks to Ebony McMillan, who serves as my personal therapist and PA on all writing projects. Lola and I depend on your kind words and encouragement. Now, stop being so selfless and get to work on writing that bestseller!

Huge thanks to my mom, retired English professor Rita Delude, who has read Lola's story from the beginning and helped me edit out her rough edges (but not too much). I wouldn't have kept her series going without you,

To those who suffer from DID and who have shared their stories with me, thank you! I see you as some of the most fascinating and brave people I've ever had the pleasure of knowing. Just because this series is over, it doesn't mean that I won't take pieces of you into my work. You are forever imprinted in both mine and Lola's heart. I hope that you continue to sparkle and shine. Your stories are not over.

Do you or someone you know have DID?

If you or someone you love have any of the signs or symptoms described below and suspect you suffer from mental illness, talk to a doctor. Treatment is available. According to the Mayo Clinic, signs and symptoms of dissociative disorders include:

- Memory loss (amnesia) of certain time periods, events and people
- Mental health problems, such as depression, anxiety, and suicidal thoughts and attempts
- A sense of being detached from yourself
- A perception of the people and things around you as distorted and unreal
- A blurred sense of identity
- Significant stress or problems in your relationships, work or other important areas of your life

There are three major dissociative disorders defined in the *Diagnostic and Statistical Manual of Mental Disorders*

(DSMV), published by the American Psychiatric Association:

- **Dissociative amnesia.** The main symptom of this disorder is memory loss that's more severe than normal forgetfulness and that can't be explained by a medical condition. You can't recall information about yourself or events and people in your life, especially from a traumatic time. Dissociative amnesia can be specific to events in a certain time, such as intense combat, or more rarely, can involve complete loss of memory about yourself. It may sometimes involve travel or confused wandering away from your life (dissociative fugue). An episode of amnesia may last minutes, hours, or, rarely, months or years.

- **Dissociative identity disorder.** This disorder, formerly known as multiple personality disorder, is characterized by "switching" to alternate identities. You may feel the presence of one or more other people talking or living inside your head, and you may feel as though you're possessed by other

identities. Each of these identities
may have a unique name, personal
history and characteristics, including
obvious differences in voice, gender,
mannerisms and even such physical
qualities as the need for eyeglasses.
There also are differences in how
familiar each identity is with the
others. People with dissociative
identity disorder typically also have
dissociative amnesia and often have
dissociative fugue.

- **Depersonalization-derealization
  disorder.** This disorder involves an
  ongoing or episodic sense of
  detachment or being outside yourself
  — observing your actions, feelings,
  thoughts and self from a distance as
  though watching a movie
  (depersonalization). Other people
  and things around you may feel
  detached and foggy or dreamlike,
  and the world may seem unreal
  (derealization). You may experience
  depersonalization, derealization or
  both. Symptoms, which can be
  profoundly distressing, may last only
  a few moments or come and go over
  many years.

Causes, Concerns and Additional Information

Dissociative disorders usually develop as a way to cope with trauma. The disorders most often form in children subjected to long-term physical, sexual or emotional abuse or, less often, a home environment that's frightening or highly unpredictable. The stress of war or natural disasters also can bring on dissociative disorders.

Personal identity is still forming during childhood. So a child is abler than an adult is to step outside of himself or herself and observe trauma as though it's happening to a different person. A child who learns to dissociate in order to endure an extended period of youth may use this coping mechanism in response to stressful situations throughout life.

People with a dissociative disorder are at increased risk of complications and associated disorders, such as:

- Self-harm
- Suicidal thoughts and attempts
- Sexual dysfunction, including sexual compulsions or avoidance

- Alcoholism and drug use disorders
- Depression and anxiety disorders
- Post-traumatic stress disorder
- Personality disorders
- Sleep disorders, including nightmares, insomnia and sleepwalking
- Eating disorders
- Severe headaches

Dissociative disorders are also associated with major difficulties in personal relationships and at work. People with these conditions often aren't able to cope well with emotional or professional stress, and their dissociative reactions—from tuning out to disappearing—may worry loved ones and cause people at work to view them as unreliable.

For a diagnosis of dissociative identity disorder, the DSM includes these criteria:

- You display, or others observe, two or more distinct identities or personalities, which may be described in some cultures as possession that is unwanted and involuntary. Each identity has its own pattern of perceiving, relating to and thinking about yourself and the world.

- You have recurrent gaps in memory for everyday events, skills, important personal information and traumatic events that are too extensive to be explained by ordinary forgetfulness.
- Your symptoms are not a part of broadly accepted cultural or religious practice.
- Your symptoms are not due to alcohol or other drugs, or a medical condition. In children, symptoms are not due to imaginary playmates or other fantasy play.
- Your symptoms cause you significant stress or problems in your relationships, work or other important areas of your life.

Psychotherapy is the primary treatment for dissociative disorders. This form of therapy, also known as talk therapy, counseling or psychosocial therapy, involves talking about your disorder and related issues with a mental health provider.

Your therapist will work to help you understand the cause of your condition and to form new ways of coping with stressful circumstances. Over time, your therapist may help you talk more about the trauma you experienced, but generally only when you have the coping skills and relationship with your therapist to safely have these conversations.

Although there are no medications that specifically treat dissociative disorders, your doctor may prescribe antidepressants, anti-anxiety medications or antipsychotic medications to help control the mental health symptoms associated with dissociative disorders.

Resources

If you have thoughts of hurting yourself or someone else, call 911 or your local emergency number immediately, go to an emergency room, or confide in a trusted relative or friend. Another option is to call a confidential suicide hotline number—in the United States, call the National Suicide Prevention Lifeline at 1-800-273-TALK (1-800-273-8255) to reach a trained counselor.

***

Information, support, and advocacy organizations:

National Alliance for the Mentally Ill (NAMI)
Colonial Place Three
2107 Wilson Blvd., Suite 300
Arlington, VA 22201-3042
Phone: 1-800-950-NAMI (6264) or (703) 524-7600
Internet: http://www.nami.org

National Mental Health Association (NMHA)
2001 N. Beauregard Street, 12th Floor
Alexandria, VA 22311

Phone: 1-800-969-6942 or (703) 684-7722
TTY-800-443-5959
Internet: http://www.nmha.org

National Mental Health Consumers' Self-Help Clearinghouse
1211 Chestnut Street, Suite 1000
Philadelphia, PA 19107
Phone: 1-800-553-4key (4539) or (215) 751-1810
Internet: http://www.mhselfhelp.org/index2.html

National Alliance for Research on Schizophrenia and Depression (NARSAD)
60 Cutter Mill Road, Suite 404
Great Neck, NY 11021
Phone: (516) 829-0091
Infoline 1-800-829-8289
Internet: http://www.narsad.org

For more information on research into the brain, behavior, and mental disorders contact:

National Institute of Mental Health (NIMH)
Office of Communication and Public Liaison

Information Resources and Inquiries
Branch
6001 Executive Boulevard, Rm. 8184,
MSC 9663
Bethesda, MD 20892-9663
Phone: 301-443-4513
Fax: 301-443-4279
E-mail: nimhinfo@nih.gov
Fax back system: Mental Health FAX4U
at 301-443-5158
Web site address:
http://www.nimh.nih.gov/

About the Author

Erin Lee is a freelance writer and therapist chasing a crazy dream one crazy story at a time. She lives with her family in southern New Hampshire. She is the author of *Crazy Like Me*, a novel published in 2015 by Savant Books and Publications, LLC, reprinted for ebook as *Her Kinda Crazy* in 2016, *Wave to Papa,* 2015, by Limitless Publishing and *Nine Lives* (2016). Lee is a summer indie book award winner for her novel *When I'm Dead.*

She's also author of *Alters* and *Host,* the first books in this series, and most recently the novella *Her Name Was Sam.* With the

Lola series concluded, Lee spends her nights working on upcoming novels *Love Like Crazy, (The Trouble with) Butterfly Kisses* and *99 Bottles*. On nights that she's feeling particularly brave, she works on her upcoming paranormal horror anthology piece, "Declarations" for Bonny Capps' holiday horror anthology to raise money for Shriners Children's Hospital.

Lee, whose totem animal is a butterfly, has published numerous magazine articles, particularly on the topic of mental illness. She recently contributed to the *Anonymous* anthology, in support of the Semi Colon Project with her short story "One Good Reason." Her short story psychological thriller, "Rest in Peace?" is featured in Limitless' *13* anthology in support of mental wellness. Her short story, "Daddy's Little Monster" is featured in Jaded Press Publishing's *Black Candy* anthology. She holds a master's degree in psychology and works with at-risk families and as a court appointed special advocate.

More on Erin Lee's work can be found at www.authorerinlee.com, and on Goodreads under Author Erin Lee and on Twitter at @Crazylikeme2015.

***

Final note from Erin with her pesky therapy hat on, *again*:

We are *all* a little crazy. If you or someone you know is struggling with a mental illness, please reach out for help. You are far from alone. Life is hard. Change, even good change, is even harder. Your story isn't over. Keep penning the pages of your own life. Only you can tell and define your own story. Find your happy ending. It's there if you are willing to try.

***

***

***

ISBN-13: 978-1533413215

ISBN-10: 1533413215

Enjoy this Series?
Check out this excerpt from
ERIN LEE's latest novella, *Her*
Name Was Sam, **now available on**
amazon:

Red

Red is the color of blood. I try not to think about it. I refuse to look at my own hands. If I did, they'd be covered in it. I hate red.

***

Kelly

I stand in a sea of color. It's so bright, so real, that I feel like I could almost reach out and taste it. I imagine it tastes like summer's fat watermelon slices or the Fourth of July. But my mouth is dry. Even if I could, I wouldn't take a bite. I have too much guilt. The only reason I'm standing here is because I helped kill my daughter. If I'm totally honest with you, and with myself, I would never be standing here if Sam hadn't done what she did.

She asked me to come with her to this very parade so many times. I told her there was no way I'd be caught dead marching down the streets like this. I tried to convince her it was just a phase. I told her to keep an open mind, the very thing she was asking of me. I said she was just curious and experimenting. I even tried to tell her it was all a normal part of growing up. But deep down, I knew. I knew exactly what was going on with her. I also knew how important it was to her that I support her. I just wasn't ready. I couldn't see myself as "that" mom. The last thing I wanted to have was pride.

I couldn't understand why she couldn't be normal. I felt like she was only doing it to punish me. I'd watch her, getting dressed in wild patterns and heels so high I was sure she'd twist an ankle. She'd put on so much make-up it reminded me of a circus clown. I told her so. I told her to take off the mask. She glared at me, telling me I didn't understand.

It's ironic that I'm here now. Being at the rainbow parade is a horrible consolation prize. I only want my daughter back. I'd go to a parade like every year for the rest of my life if I could change things. I'd even have pride: In her. In me. In a million things I wouldn't have done so awfully wrong. Pride in the things I'd do-over. Do right.

I wonder what she thinks of me today and almost hope there's no afterlife. I admit it, I'm a hypocrite. I should have been here years ago. I should have done whatever it took to support her. But there are no do overs. At least, I don't think.

Sam believed in reincarnation. She's probably too busy living another, better life, to be paying attention. If she is, I know she's rolling her eyes. She'd say, "Finally, Mom's here."

The ironic thing is, I couldn't *not* be here. I am, after all, a conspirator. Maybe I can help some other mother from suffering the same fate. Sam always used to say, "Everything happens for a reason."

I can't imagine a good enough reason for her suicide. But there were many. I might have been able to stop her, had I listened. I didn't listen when she told me how bad the bullying had become. I didn't take her seriously or buy her the new dresses and make-up she asked for. I told her she needed to see a therapist and to stop trying to change who she was. I said that she needed to focus on school and ignore everyone around her. I told her she was too young to date and that the only thing that would solve her problems was prayer. I even asked her what the neighbors might think.

Sure, there were warning signs. I should have paid closer attention when her grades dropped and she stopped attending band practice. I should have known something was wrong when she burnt her journals in the backyard. I let her give her trumpet and flute away. Instead, I wrote it off to teen angst and told myself she was only going through another phase. I painted over her pink walls and made them blue. I figured it might help her rethink things.

It's probably a good thing that I can't hear myself think. A man wearing white leggings and rainbow leg warmers has a gold horn on his head. His mohawk is dyed every color of the rainbow. I think he's supposed to be a unicorn. I try not to wince as he spins and twirls and prances by. I tell myself at least his mother has him alive.

Someday, I hope to be able to smile with him. I hope to be able to look past the glitter and overt cries of "pride". For now, I need to just be here, part of it, and try. Three young girls, with their arms locked together, march beside me. Their faces are painted red and I wonder what it symbolizes. They laugh and smile and I have to make myself look away. It's too late.

"Hi! I'm Aubree!" The tallest of the three, the one to the far right, smiles at me. "And this is Harley and Sue."

I smile back and keep marching forward. I don't know what to say. I remind myself of what Sam used to say— "They're just like everyone else, Ma. Just people, too."

"Hi. I'm Kelly."

Aubree snaps her gum. I can smell the grape from two feet away. Now, my smile is sincere. Sam liked anything and everything fruity. Skittles, grape, were her favorite. And don't get me started on her love for Starburst. The girl could eat five packages in one sitting.

"First time?" Sue, the roundest of the three, looks me up and down.

I have second thoughts about the PRIDE tee shirt I bought at the start of the parade. *She can see right through me.* I nod.

"Cool."

"Yeah, thanks," I say, wishing I'd brought Morgan along. She'd know what to do. Morgan has been dealing with this for years.

"You here alone?"

I shrug. "Sort of."

"Sort of?"

"Well. Yes. I guess I'm here alone."

"Cool."

"Thanks." *Awkward.*

"What do you mean, sort of?" It's the first time Harley has spoken. Her enormous green eyes don't seem threatening; instead, inquisitive, as she shifts between the two other girls and unlocks her arms to wipe sweat from her forehead.

"I guess. Well. I like to think my daughter is here with me."

"Where is she?"

You practically begged her to ask. Answer the poor thing. Or, maybe, lie. No one wants to hear that. And they will know you killed her. "She's not here."

I catch a squint in Harley's eyes as she looks to each of her friends for some explanation they may have picked up on. They shrug and smile.

"Cool," Aubree finally says, and keeps marching. "Hey! Look! A cheetah!"

I walk a little slower, letting them get ahead of me. From behind, they seem like any other teenage girls. I want to catch back up and ask them where their mothers are. I wonder if their mother's even know. Or, why it even matters. *Stop thinking so much. You're here to support Sam. That is all. And, it's not enough.*

I never got to see Sam with a girlfriend. Morgan says there was one. I have a feeling she was right. There was a girl, one who looked a lot like Aubree, at her funeral. She sobbed a little longer and lingered in front of a picture of Sam in her favorite yellow hat. *That girl must have been her.*

What would Sam look like in love? I imagine her smile even brighter than it often was. When she was little, she talked about her wedding day. She said bridesmaids would wear yellow and there would be daisy crowns for everyone. She wanted to get married on the ocean. Or, on a farm. Sam never could fully make up her mind. Maybe it was just that there were so many things she wanted to do and experience.

I wonder what Sam would have been like as a mother. I've even thought about what it would be like for her to have an LGBTQ child of her own. She would have known what to do and never missed a parade. In fact, she would have organized the parade. Sam always did like taking charge.

These are the things I'll never know. I don't think a day goes by where I don't contemplate who Sam was and might have been. The funny thing about regret is that it never really leaves you; not until you make peace with it. Right now, I'm stuck on regretting regret. I have a long way to go.

But then, what else better do I have to do? For me, falling in love again, having more kids, and even planning weddings, just aren't in the cards anymore. Morgan says she'll never get married. I believe her. She's too messed up to get attached to anyone. I don't blame her. She's had too many losses for a kid her age. She's had enough. I get it.

Morgan is what keeps me going. Without her, Sam would have company. It's another thing I think about a lot; alone at night drinking myself to sleep. If only, I always think, I had the same kind of courage as my daughter.

Her name was Sam. She was beautiful in every way. She could light up a room even on her saddest day. She loved to sing and dance and played any instrument she could get her hands on. She was never afraid to hit a wrong note. She just wanted to make music. Sam lived to make other people happy. She liked to entertain. She couldn't have been four when she made my kitchen into a concert hall and wouldn't let me have my pots back for months. For an entire summer, I had to make do with an electric skillet. "Don't mess up my band, Ma!"

Her name was Sam and all she really wanted was to be seen and heard. I'll never forget the look on her face the first time she grew her hair out long enough to tie it back. It was utterly ridiculous. But, to Sam, she looked like the queen of the world and wanted everyone to know. She had two stumps sticking out of her blonde head on either side. They reminded me of antlers.

"Look, Ma! Pony tails!" She twirled round my kitchen and I was mortified. A neighbor had just come over to borrow eggs. The neighbor was mortified too, at least when Sam stuck her tongue out at her for what appeared to be no reason. "I need five spoons and a wooden bowl. We're making a fort and doing make overs. Do you have nail polish?"

"Sam! Take that out of your hair and go get cleaned up! And those *aren't* pony tails! Pony tails are long and flowy. Those are, maybe, pig tails. Take them out," I barked, praying Mrs. Johnson wouldn't repeat what she'd seen to the neighbors at the block party. (Fortunately, she didn't. But she never looked at me quite the same and suddenly never needed to borrow a single egg). "And you're being *rude*, Sam! Say hello to Mrs. Johnson."

"No way! She's mean, too! And they *are* ponytails! You're so *mean*!" Sam yelled, stomping back outside to play. "Come on, Morgan! Let's go make a girl's fort. We can make a sign that says 'no meanie pants Mom's allowed!'"

"I don't want to play with you," Morgan said. "I want to stay here with Mom and make brownies."

"Gross. You are dumb."

"Sam!"

"Well, she is! She's a brown nose. And boring too!"

"Well you aren't going anywhere until you apologize to Mrs. Johnson for being rude."

Sam planted her feet firmly into the kitchen tile. With her arms crossed, I knew there was no arguing with her. I was relieved when Mrs. Johnson excused herself; but terrified about what she might do all at the same time.

It seems too silly now, that I even worried about these things. Years later, Mrs. Johnson had problems of her own when her son was arrested for burglary. I wonder what she'd think if she knew Sam had been the first to defend him; saying everyone had their reasons for doing what they did. "Don't judge, Ma. You never know."

Her name was Sam, and I didn't really know her. At least not until it was too late… Maybe here, at the PRIDE parade, I can find more clues. Now, there's nothing I don't want to know.

***

Sam

My name is Sam. I've been dead for almost a year. I killed myself because I couldn't take it anymore. Sure, it's ugly. It's horrible. It was probably selfish, too. But I didn't feel like I had a choice. I was tired of hurting everyone around me. I felt like they would be better off with me gone. Watching them, I know, they probably are.

My mother attended her first PRIDE parade today. That's a regret I have, I guess. I would have loved to have gone with her— in my body, I mean. I wish I could tell her how proud I am of her. And of Morgan, my sister, who is stuck dealing with this mess at school. Morgan, the baby, who has to grow up too fast because of me. I can't think about it.

For years, I begged my mother to understand. She just wasn't ready. I know she believed me; that I was just being true to myself. She just wished it could be different. The truth is, I did too. But I never regretted it, being true to who I was. I just didn't want to cause more pain.

If I could go back for just one day, there's so many things I'd say to them. I'd tell them I am alright. I'd tell them I haven't quite made sense of this thing called "afterlife," but that I'm working on it. I'd tell them they aren't alone.

There's nothing worse than feeling like you're alone. It's why I'm glad Mom has her support groups. I hope Morgan finds the same, or a boyfriend, at least. She needs people around her now. Mom's distracted. I guess I didn't think of that when I pulled the trigger.

As for Dad, he's okay, too. He has a new life, wife, and kids. I know he's sad. I mean, his first kid is dead. Who wouldn't be? But it hasn't stopped him from doing the things he enjoys. He was just out shopping for hunting gear last week.

I wonder what would have happened if I made a different choice. Would they have stood by me, or had to turn the other way? I get it that it was hard, loving me. People stared and called us names. Sick really, considering it wasn't something I could change.

These days, I watch over my family in a place called cloud space. I think I'm waiting for something, but I'm not sure what it is. I'd like to move fully on--to find out where my final destination will be. Patience isn't something I was ever good at. For now, I just have to have faith: Another thing I was never good at…

CRAZY
INK.